GRAPHIC SURVIVAL STORIES

DEFYING DEATH AT
SEA

by Gary Jeffrey

illustrated by Terry Riley

rosen publishing's
rosen central®

New York

Published in 2010 by The Rosen Publishing Group, Inc.
29 East 21st Street, New York, NY 10010

Designed and produced by
David West Books

Editor: Katharine Pethick

Photo credits:
P4t, Rear Admiral Harley D. Nygren, NOAA Corps (ret.); 5m, NOAA; 5r, -just-jen-; 5b, Mila Zinkova; 5br, Nick Hobgood; 6t, Courtesy of the U.S. Navy Art Collection, Washington, DC.; 6m, P. Ubriaco; 6b, Val Gempis; 7m, foxypar4; 7b, Andy Murch diver photographer; 44, loop_oh; 45t, Tim Patterson; 45b, wsweet321

Library of Congress Cataloging-in-Publication Data

Jeffrey, Gary.
 Defying death at sea / Gary Jeffrey ; illustrated by Terry Riley. -- 1st ed.
    p. cm. -- (Graphic survival stories)
 Includes index.
 ISBN 978-1-4358-3530-6 (library binding) -- ISBN 978-1-61532-863-5 (pbk.) -- ISBN 978-1-61532-864-2 (6-pack)
 1. Marine accidents--Juvenile literature. 2. Survival after airplane accidents, shipwrecks, etc--Juvenile literature. I. Riley, Terry, ill. II. Title.
 G525.J4447 2010
 910.4'52--dc22

                                           2009039485

Manufactured in China

CPSIA Compliance Information: Batch #DW0102YA:
For Further Information contact Rosen Publishing, New York, New York at 1-800-237-9932

CONTENTS

THE WORLD'S OCEANS

ARCTIC OCEAN

Almost three-quarters of the Earth's surface is covered with salt water. The oceans worldwide contain a wealth of environments and life-forms. Important for travel and economics, the ocean also has a major effect on the world's climate.

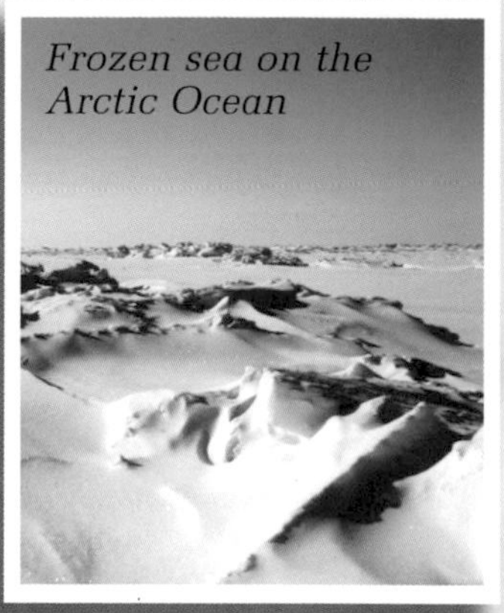

Frozen sea on the Arctic Ocean

OCEAN ZONES

Largest of the five oceans, the Pacific could hold all the land of the Earth with room to spare. Like the Atlantic, it is divided into north and south zones by the equator. The third largest division is the Indian Ocean, which lies south of Asia and west of Africa. Crowning the world is the the fourth and smallest zone, the Arctic Ocean. The Southern Ocean surrounds Antarctica.

ATLANTIC OCEAN

PACIFIC OCEAN

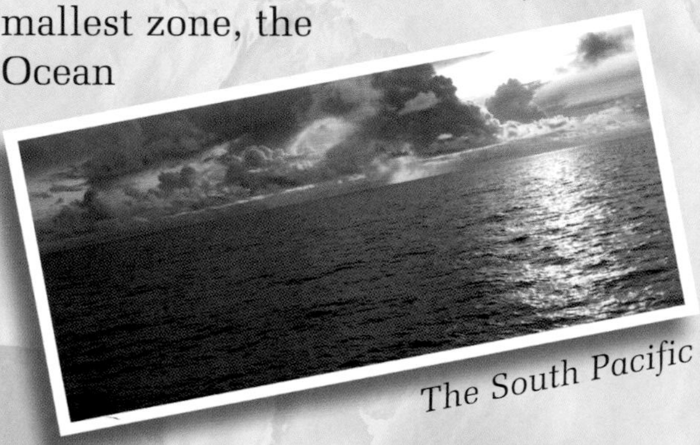

The South Pacific

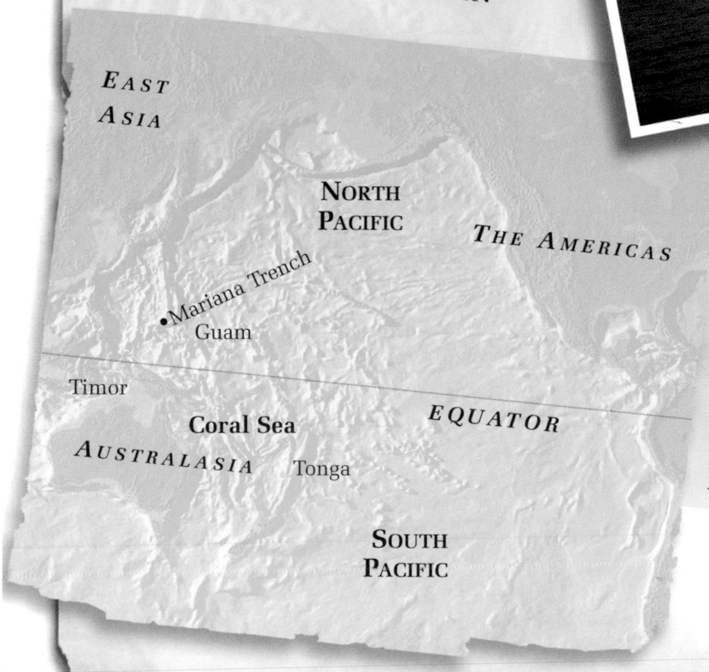
EAST ASIA
NORTH PACIFIC
THE AMERICAS
Mariana Trench
Guam
Timor
Coral Sea
EQUATOR
AUSTRALASIA
Tonga
SOUTH PACIFIC

The Pacific was named by 16th-century Portuguese explorer Ferdinand Magellan because of its apparent stillness (although it can be anything but!). It has more islands than the other four oceans put together, and contains the lowest point on Earth—the Mariana Trench, which is 6.7 miles (10.9 km) deep.

SOUTHERN OCEAN

The Atlantic was the first ocean to be discovered and explored by western Europeans. It has some of the world's busiest shipping lanes and some of its richest fishing grounds. The mid-Atlantic is where hurricanes are formed.

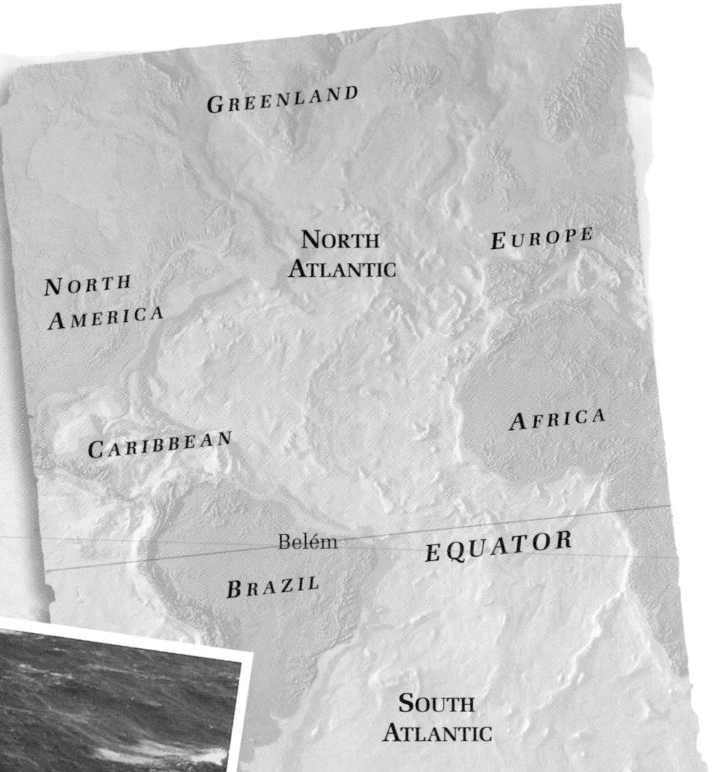

GREENLAND
NORTH ATLANTIC
EUROPE
NORTH AMERICA
AFRICA
CARIBBEAN
Belém
EQUATOR
BRAZIL
SOUTH ATLANTIC

WATERWAYS

The oceans are never still. The action of wind makes waves on the water surface and causes strong currents to circulate below. Ocean temperatures can vary from 86°F (30°C) at the equator to 28°F (-2°C) at the poles. Habitats range from the cold emptiness of the deep ocean to the warm, populous coral reefs of tropical shallows.

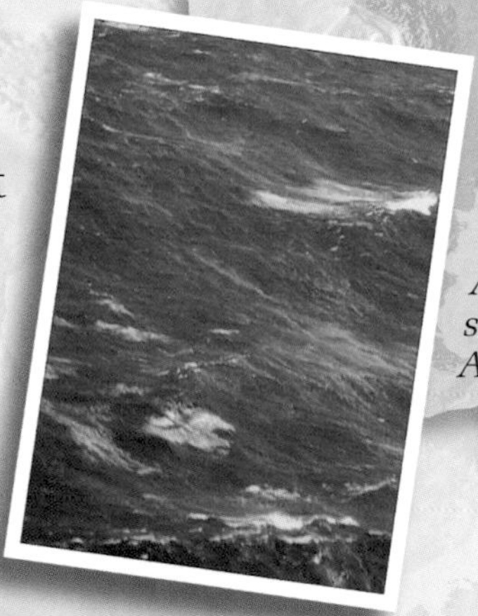

A hurricane sea in the Atlantic

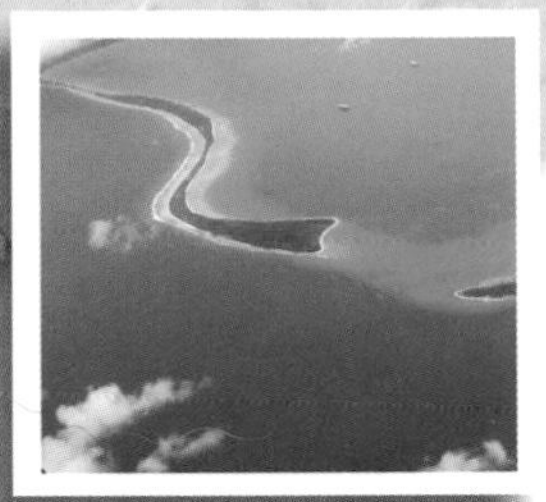

Islands in the Indian Ocean

INDAN OCEAN

OCEANIC LIFE

Ocean-dwelling creatures range in size from microscopic plankton to whales, the largest animals on Earth, which feed on them. Multitudes of fish, crustaceans, shellfish, cephalopods, mammals, and even reptiles are adapted to live in the largest ecosystem on Earth.

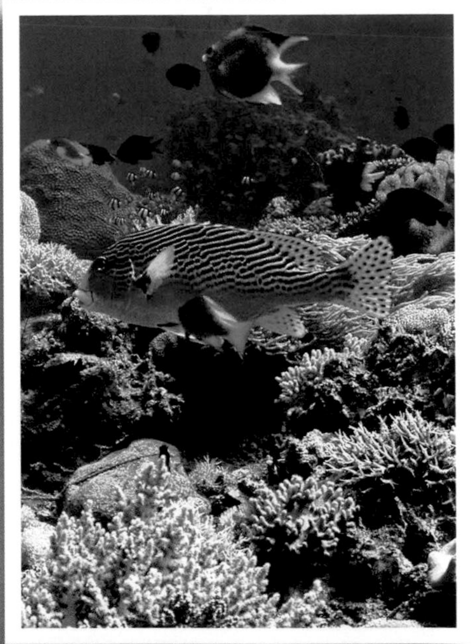

A coral reef

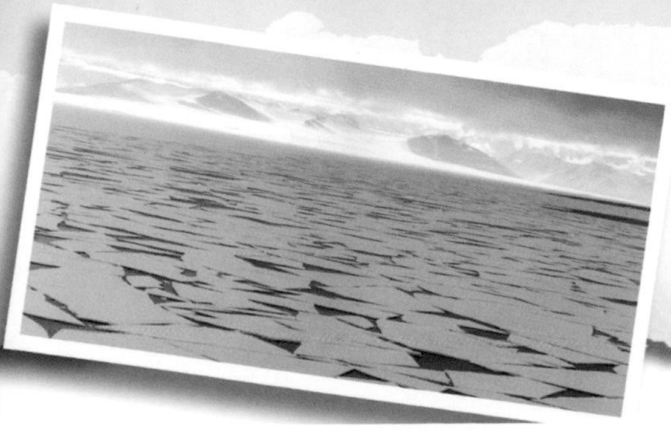

Sea ice in the Southern Ocean

SURVIVAL AT SEA

Most of us who travel will at some point cross a large body of water. Being adrift on the ocean is arguably the most challenging survival situation of all.

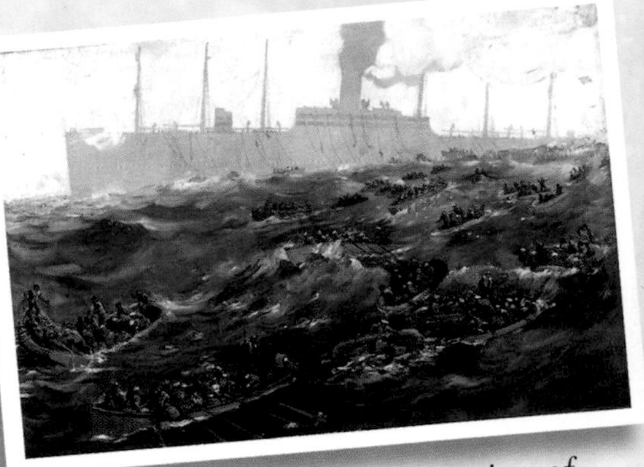

"Abandon ship!" The beginning of every seafarer's nightmare

On the Water

Survival and rescue depends on equipment available, initiative used, and strength of will to live. On the vast, featureless ocean the elements rule. Sunburn, heatstroke, or death from cold are constant dangers, along with dehydration.

Although it's all around, salt water is *not* safe to drink. It will quickly overload the body's kidneys, causing all cells to expel their water in an effort to cleanse the body of sodium. This is irreversible. Dementia and death will follow.

Rationing supplies of freshwater stores and collecting rainwater is of paramount importance at sea.

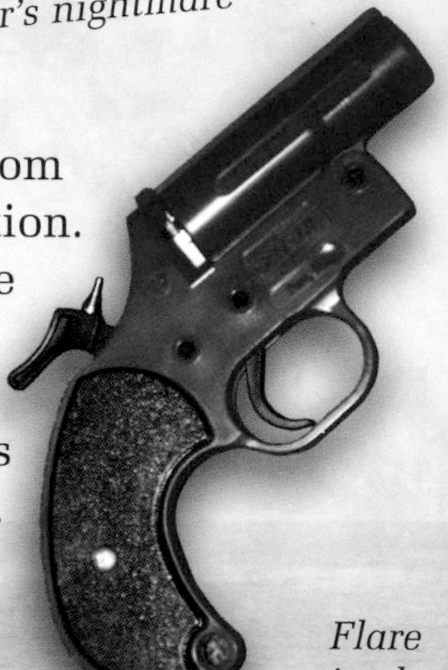

Flare pistols are sometimes included in lifeboat emergency kits.

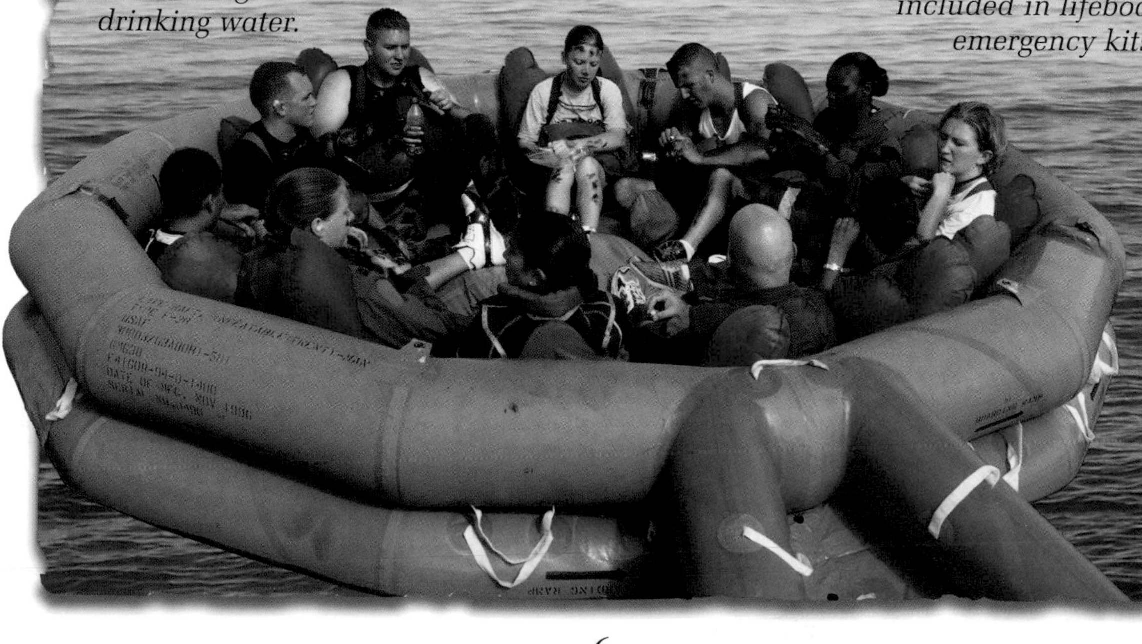

Survivors in a raft will have a decent chance—if they have enough drinking water.

SURVIVAL TIPS

- **TRY TO STAY NEAR WHERE YOU WENT IN.** Rescuers will head for your last known location first.
- **TIE LIFE RAFTS TOGETHER** so they will be easier to spot from the air.
- **TRY TO RELAX.** You will consume less energy (difficult in a storm).
- **REDUCE SWEATING** in the tropics by soaking clothes in seawater and wringing them out before wearing.
- **DON'T EAT** if you are very short of water. You will use up precious fluid in your body digesting the food.
- **DRY CAUGHT FISH** that you don't immediately need, to preserve it.
- **OLD SEA ICE** in cold climates is a source of water. It is bluish in color and splinters easily. Avoid white fresh ice—it's far too salty.

In the Water

Hypothermia is when core body temperature drops so low that metabolism stops. Heat loss from the body occurs 25 times faster when submerged. Life expectancy can be measured in minutes or hours, depending on the water temperature. Skin can be corroded by immersion in salt water, causing nasty ulcers and rotten flesh.

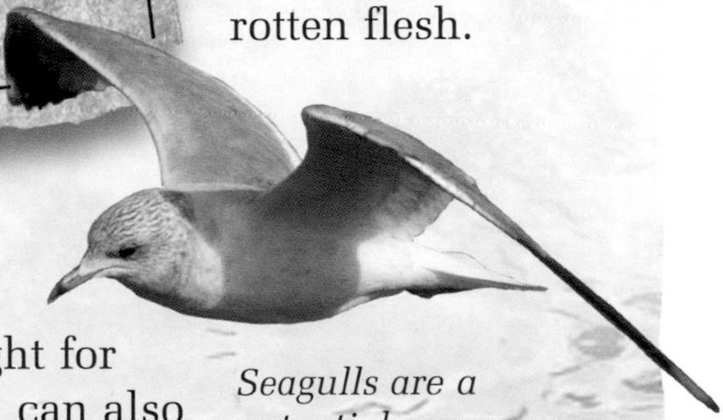

Seagulls are a potential source of food—if you can catch them.

What the Ocean Gives...and Takes

Fish, turtles, and seabirds can be caught for food, but people helpless in the ocean can also *be* food. The most dangerous ocean predators are sharks. Sharks will usually feed off the dead and dying first. Cautious scavengers, they will intially be wary of attacking a healthy adult human. However, after a few days of circling they may become bolder.

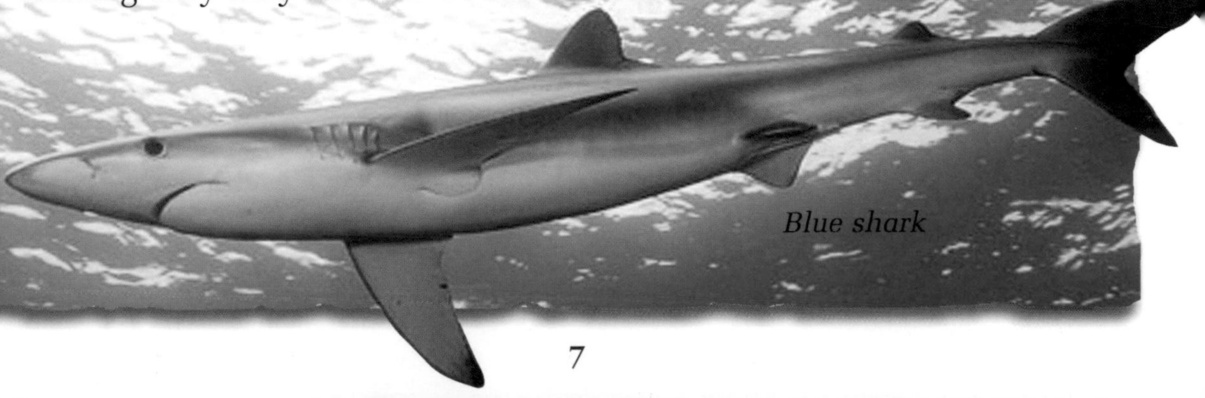

Blue shark

MUTINY ON THE BOUNTY

ENGLISH LIEUTENANT WILLIAM BLIGH & CREW, NEAR THE ISLAND OF TONGA, SOUTH PACIFIC, APRIL 28, 1789

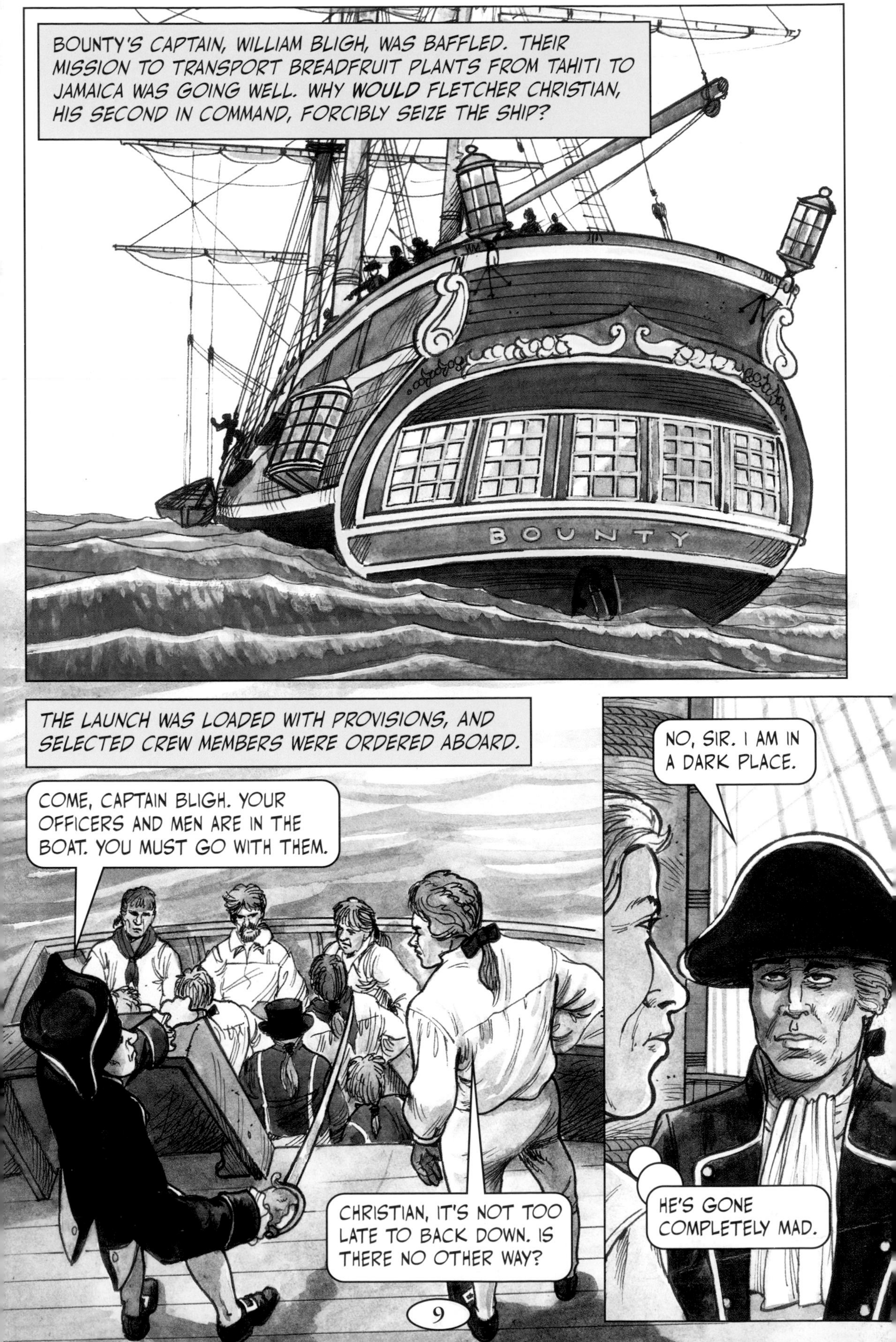
BOUNTY'S CAPTAIN, WILLIAM BLIGH, WAS BAFFLED. THEIR MISSION TO TRANSPORT BREADFRUIT PLANTS FROM TAHITI TO JAMAICA WAS GOING WELL. WHY WOULD FLETCHER CHRISTIAN, HIS SECOND IN COMMAND, FORCIBLY SEIZE THE SHIP?
BOUNTY
THE LAUNCH WAS LOADED WITH PROVISIONS, AND SELECTED CREW MEMBERS WERE ORDERED ABOARD.
COME, CAPTAIN BLIGH. YOUR OFFICERS AND MEN ARE IN THE BOAT. YOU MUST GO WITH THEM.
CHRISTIAN, IT'S NOT TOO LATE TO BACK DOWN. IS THERE NO OTHER WAY?
NO, SIR. I AM IN A DARK PLACE.
HE'S GONE COMPLETELY MAD.

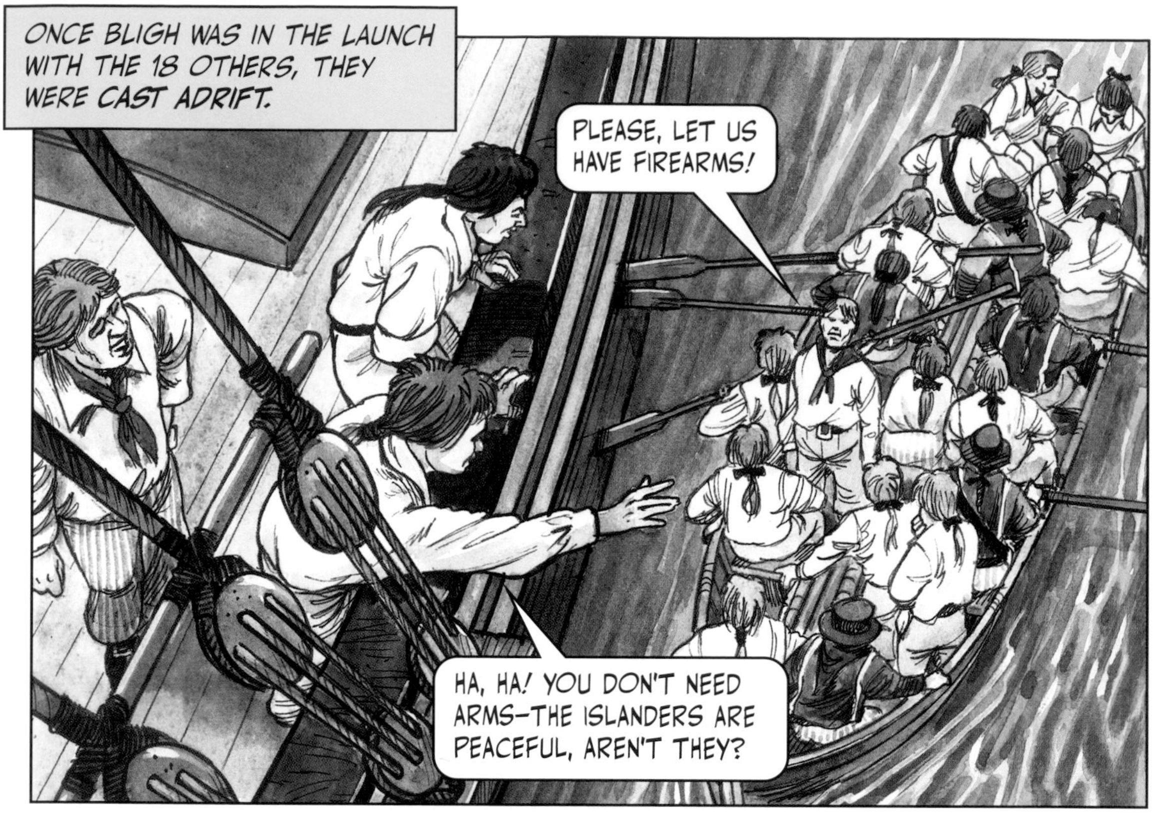
ONCE BLIGH WAS IN THE LAUNCH WITH THE 18 OTHERS, THEY WERE CAST ADRIFT.
PLEASE, LET US HAVE FIREARMS!
HA, HA! YOU DON'T NEED ARMS—THE ISLANDERS ARE PEACEFUL, AREN'T THEY?

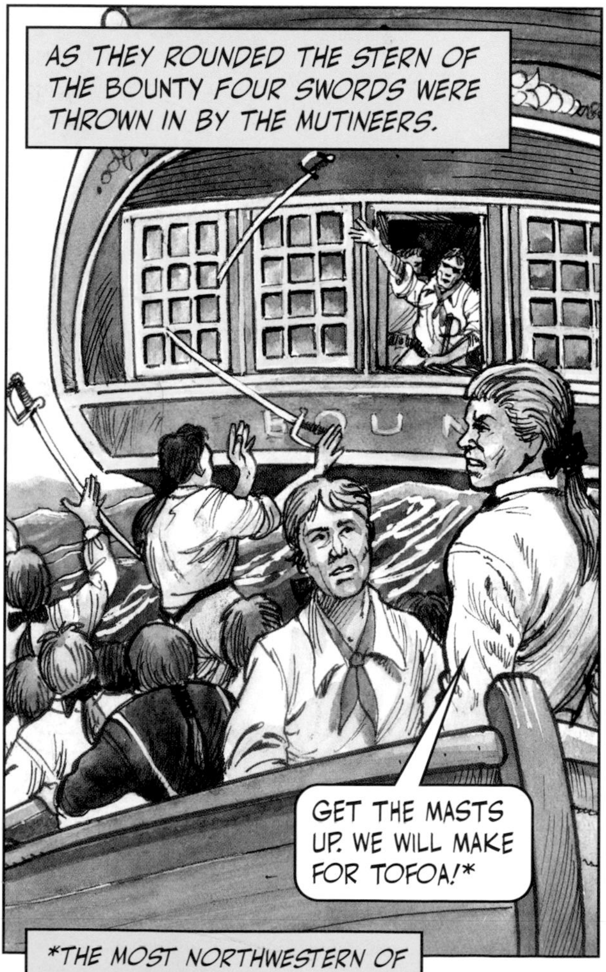
AS THEY ROUNDED THE STERN OF THE BOUNTY FOUR SWORDS WERE THROWN IN BY THE MUTINEERS.
GET THE MASTS UP. WE WILL MAKE FOR TOFOA!*
*THE MOST NORTHWESTERN OF THE "FRIENDLY" ISLES

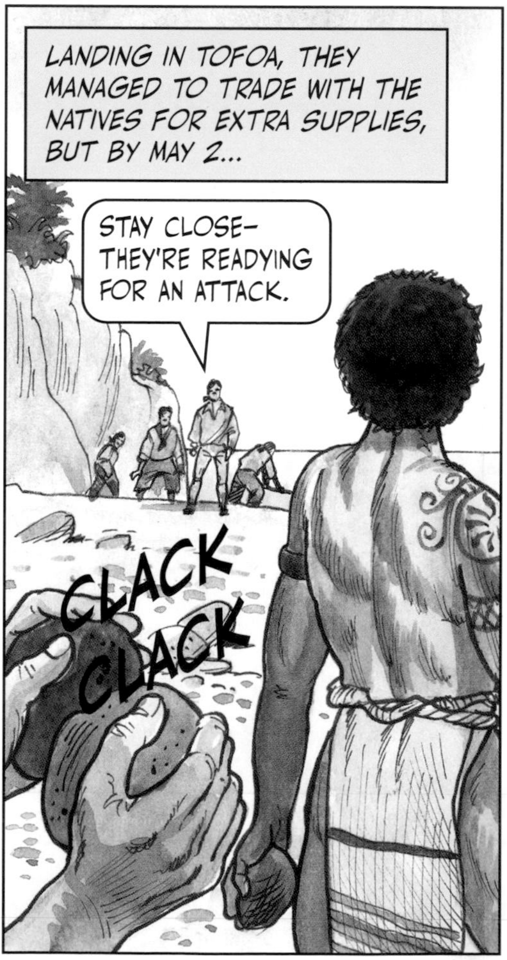
LANDING IN TOFOA, THEY MANAGED TO TRADE WITH THE NATIVES FOR EXTRA SUPPLIES, BUT BY MAY 2...
STAY CLOSE— THEY'RE READYING FOR AN ATTACK.
CLACK
CLACK

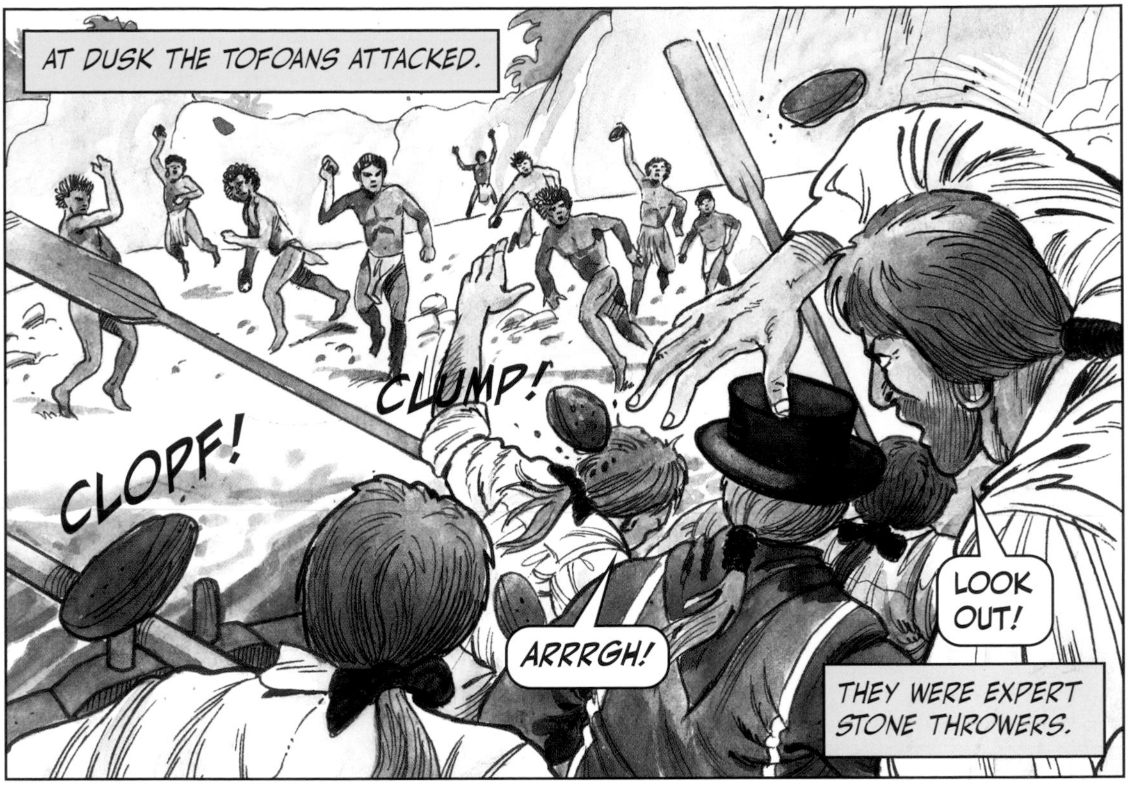
AT DUSK THE TOFOANS ATTACKED.
CLUMP!
CLOPF!
ARRRGH!
LOOK OUT!
THEY WERE EXPERT STONE THROWERS.

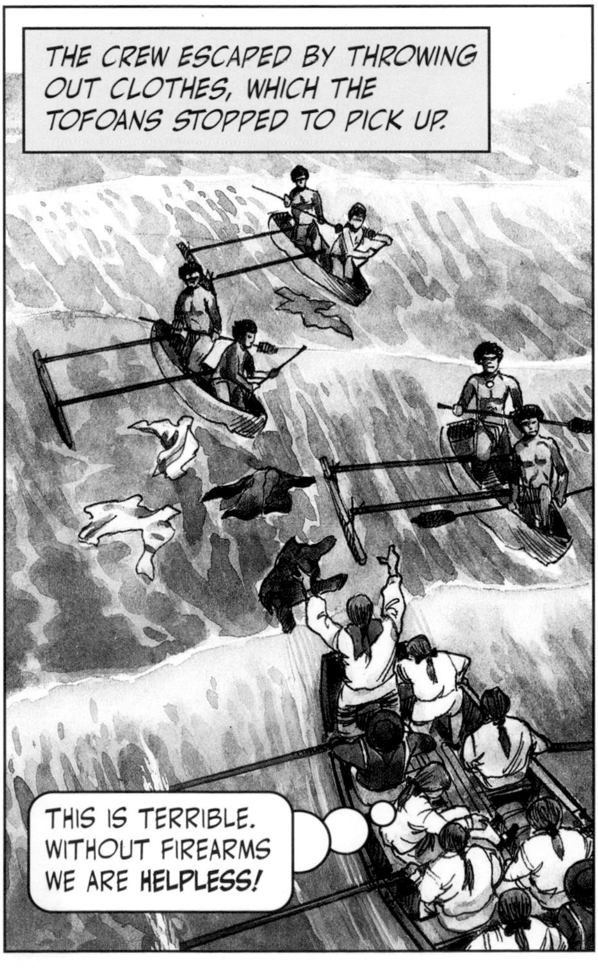
THE CREW ESCAPED BY THROWING OUT CLOTHES, WHICH THE TOFOANS STOPPED TO PICK UP.
THIS IS TERRIBLE. WITHOUT FIREARMS WE ARE **HELPLESS!**

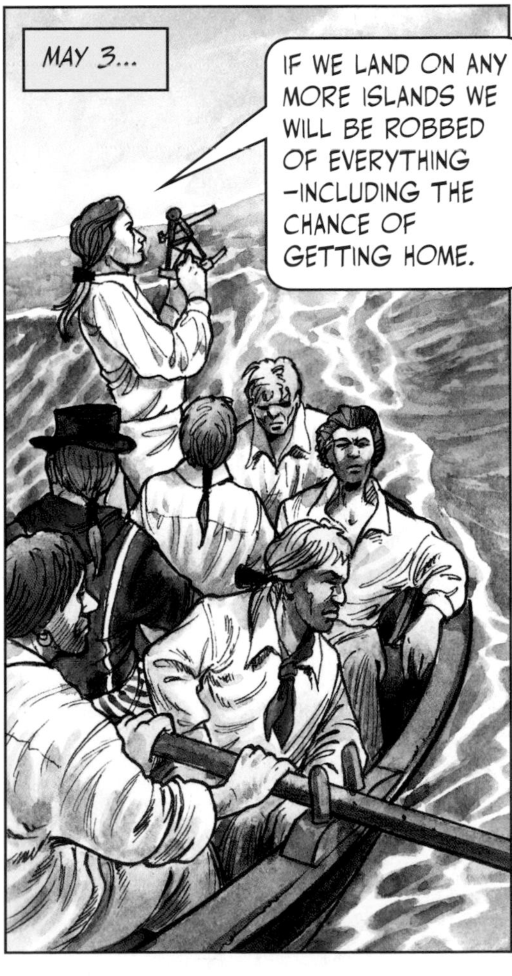
MAY 3...
IF WE LAND ON ANY MORE ISLANDS WE WILL BE ROBBED OF EVERYTHING –INCLUDING THE CHANCE OF GETTING HOME.

OUR BEST HOPE IS TO SAIL TO TIMOR, TWELVE HUNDRED LEAGUES* DISTANT.

*4,200 MILES (6,759 KM)

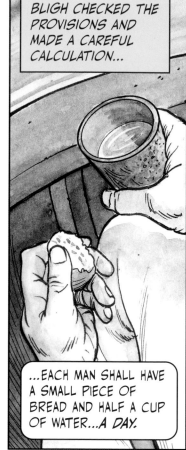

BLIGH CHECKED THE PROVISIONS AND MADE A CAREFUL CALCULATION...

...EACH MAN SHALL HAVE A SMALL PIECE OF BREAD AND HALF A CUP OF WATER...*A DAY.*

ADDED TO THESE RATIONS WERE SOME SALT PORK, COCONUTS, AND RUM. BLIGH FIGURED IT WOULD TAKE THEM EIGHT WEEKS TO COMPLETE THEIR JOURNEY...

...*IF* WE ARE LUCKY.

THEY SAILED NORTHWEST, SOMETIMES ROWING AROUND REEFS, CAREFUL TO STAY AWAY FROM THE NUMEROUS ISLANDS THEY ENCOUNTERED.

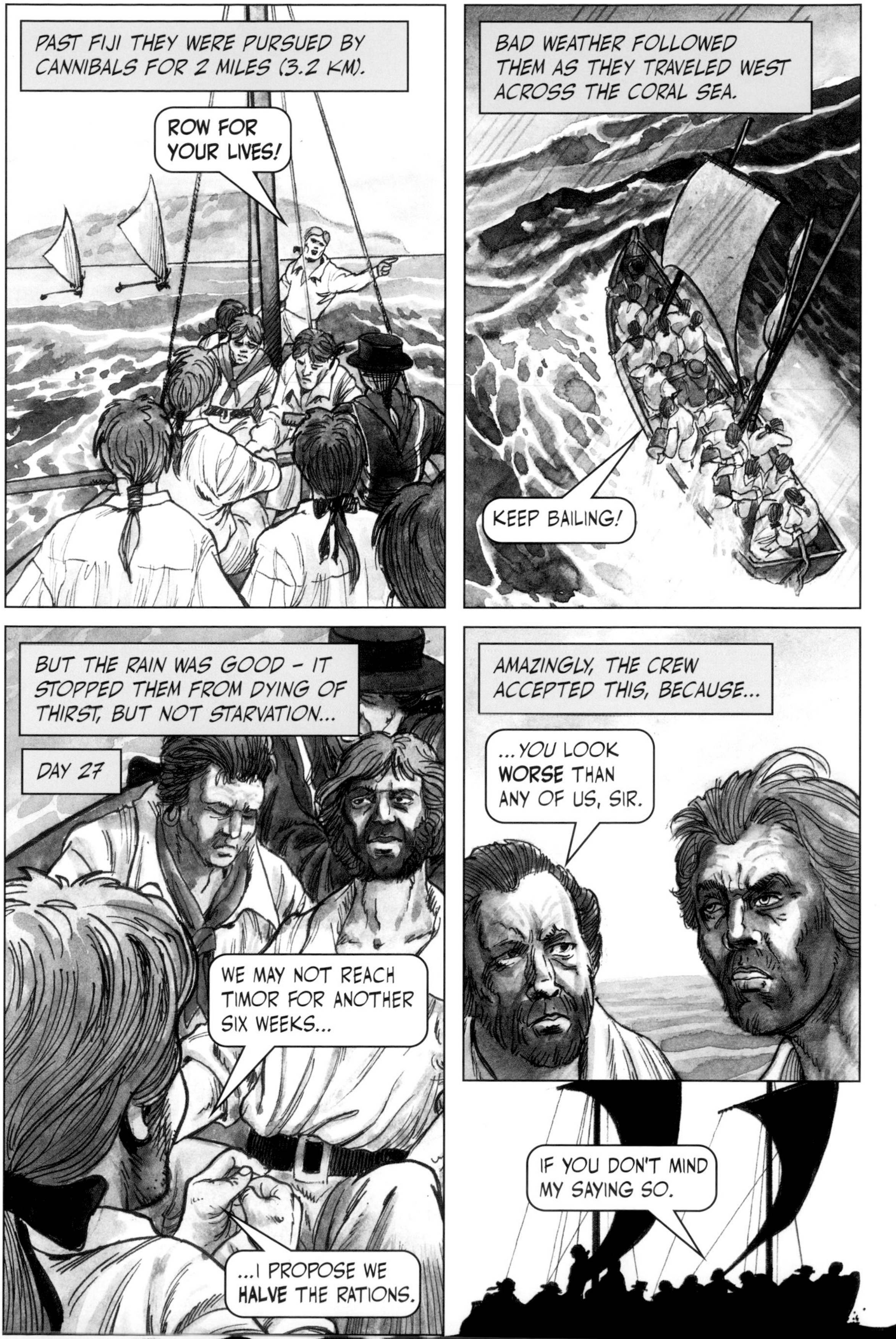
PAST FIJI THEY WERE PURSUED BY CANNIBALS FOR 2 MILES (3.2 KM).
ROW FOR YOUR LIVES!
BAD WEATHER FOLLOWED THEM AS THEY TRAVELED WEST ACROSS THE CORAL SEA.
KEEP BAILING!
BUT THE RAIN WAS GOOD - IT STOPPED THEM FROM DYING OF THIRST, BUT NOT STARVATION...
DAY 27
WE MAY NOT REACH TIMOR FOR ANOTHER SIX WEEKS...
...I PROPOSE WE HALVE THE RATIONS.
AMAZINGLY, THE CREW ACCEPTED THIS, BECAUSE...
...YOU LOOK WORSE THAN ANY OF US, SIR.
IF YOU DON'T MIND MY SAYING SO.

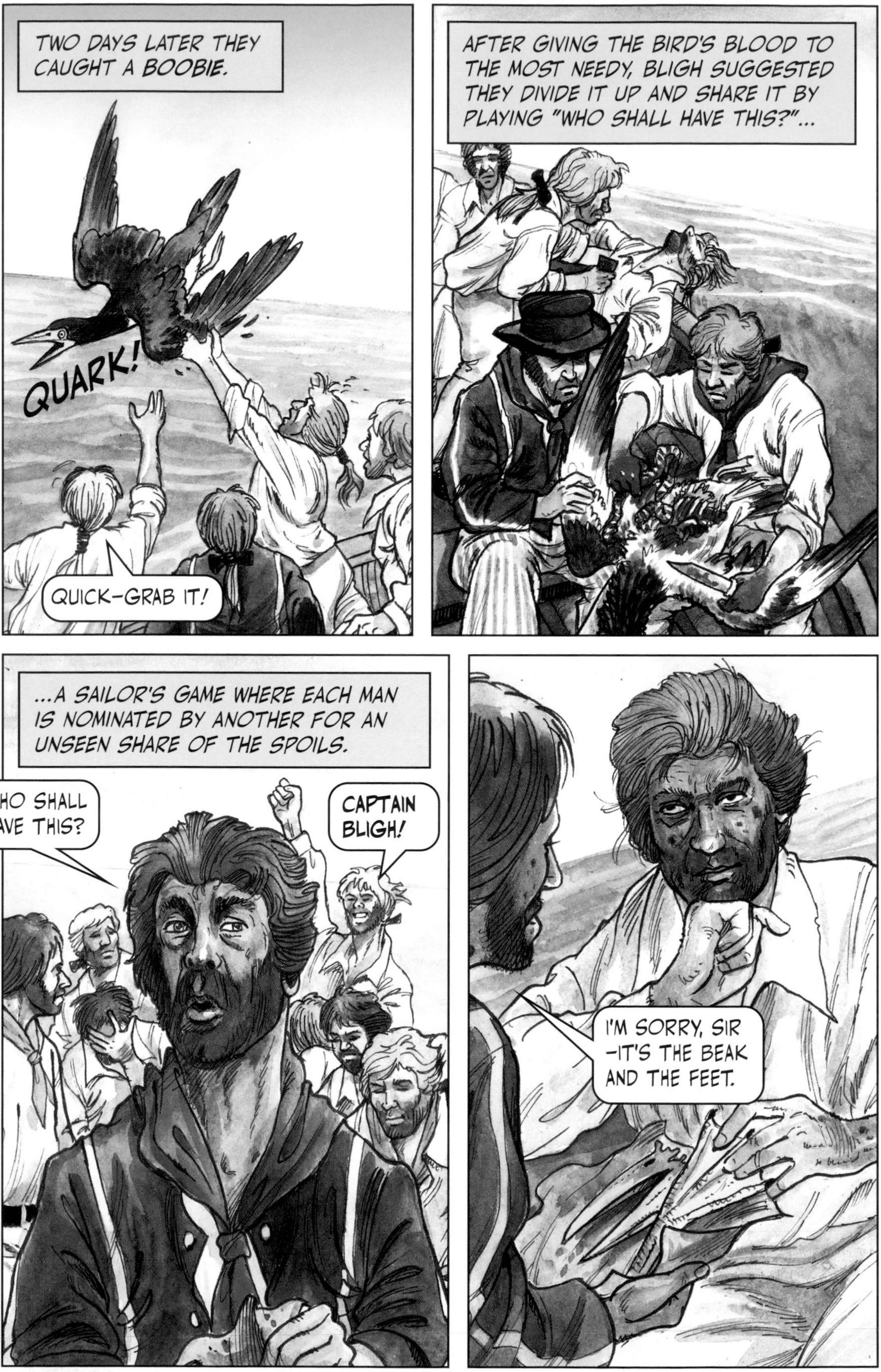
TWO DAYS LATER THEY CAUGHT A BOOBIE.
QUARK!
QUICK-GRAB IT!
AFTER GIVING THE BIRD'S BLOOD TO THE MOST NEEDY, BLIGH SUGGESTED THEY DIVIDE IT UP AND SHARE IT BY PLAYING "WHO SHALL HAVE THIS?"...
...A SAILOR'S GAME WHERE EACH MAN IS NOMINATED BY ANOTHER FOR AN UNSEEN SHARE OF THE SPOILS.
WHO SHALL HAVE THIS?
CAPTAIN BLIGH!
I'M SORRY, SIR -IT'S THE BEAK AND THE FEET.

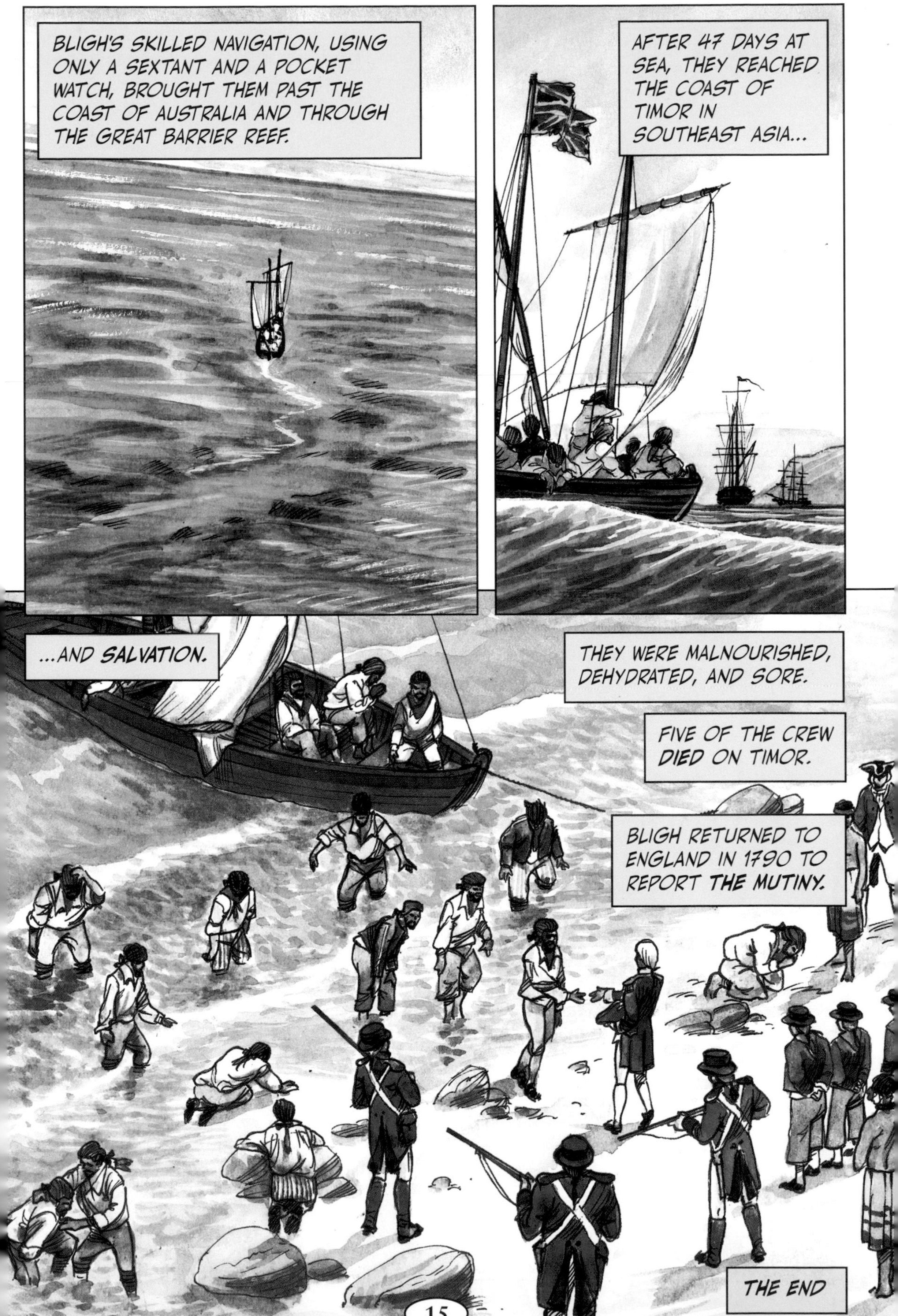
BLIGH'S SKILLED NAVIGATION, USING ONLY A SEXTANT AND A POCKET WATCH, BROUGHT THEM PAST THE COAST OF AUSTRALIA AND THROUGH THE GREAT BARRIER REEF.
AFTER 47 DAYS AT SEA, THEY REACHED THE COAST OF TIMOR IN SOUTHEAST ASIA...
...AND SALVATION.
THEY WERE MALNOURISHED, DEHYDRATED, AND SORE.
FIVE OF THE CREW DIED ON TIMOR.
BLIGH RETURNED TO ENGLAND IN 1790 TO REPORT THE MUTINY.
THE END

LOST AT SEA ON A LIFE RAFT

Chinese Merchant Sailor Poon Lim, West Africa, South Atlantic, November 23, 1942

*SEEN THROUGH THE PERISCOPE OF GERMAN SUBMARINE U-172, THE UNESCORTED MERCHANT SHIP IS TOO **TEMPTING** A TARGET TO **RESIST**...*

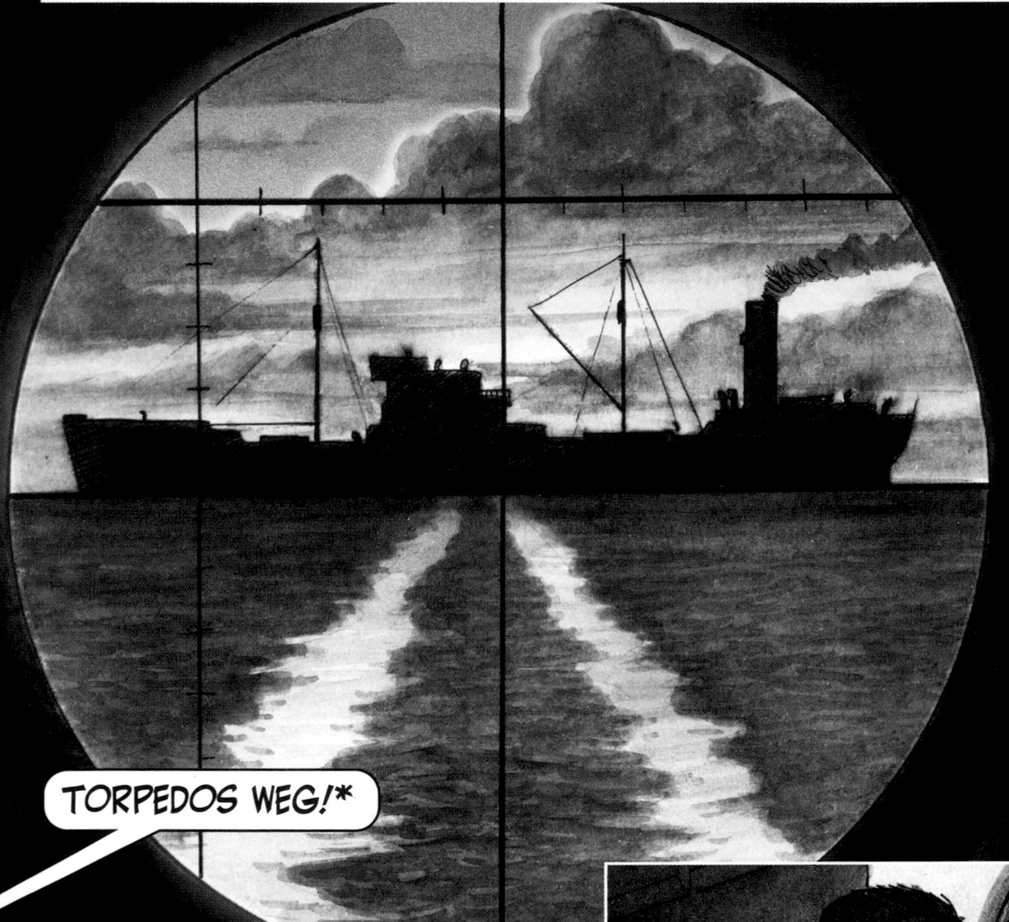
TORPEDOS WEG!*

**TORPEDOES AWAY!*

*ON BOARD THE SS BEN LOMOND, SECOND STEWARD POON LIM IS ALONE ON DECK. LOOKING UP, HE SEES THE **WAKE** OF THE TORPEDOES GLISTENING IN THE MOONLIGHT.*

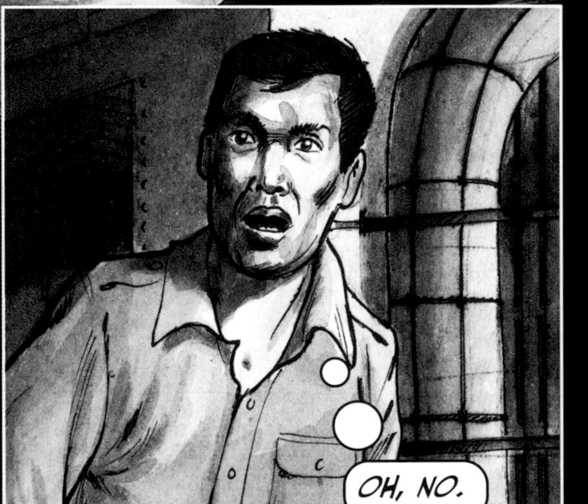
OH, NO.

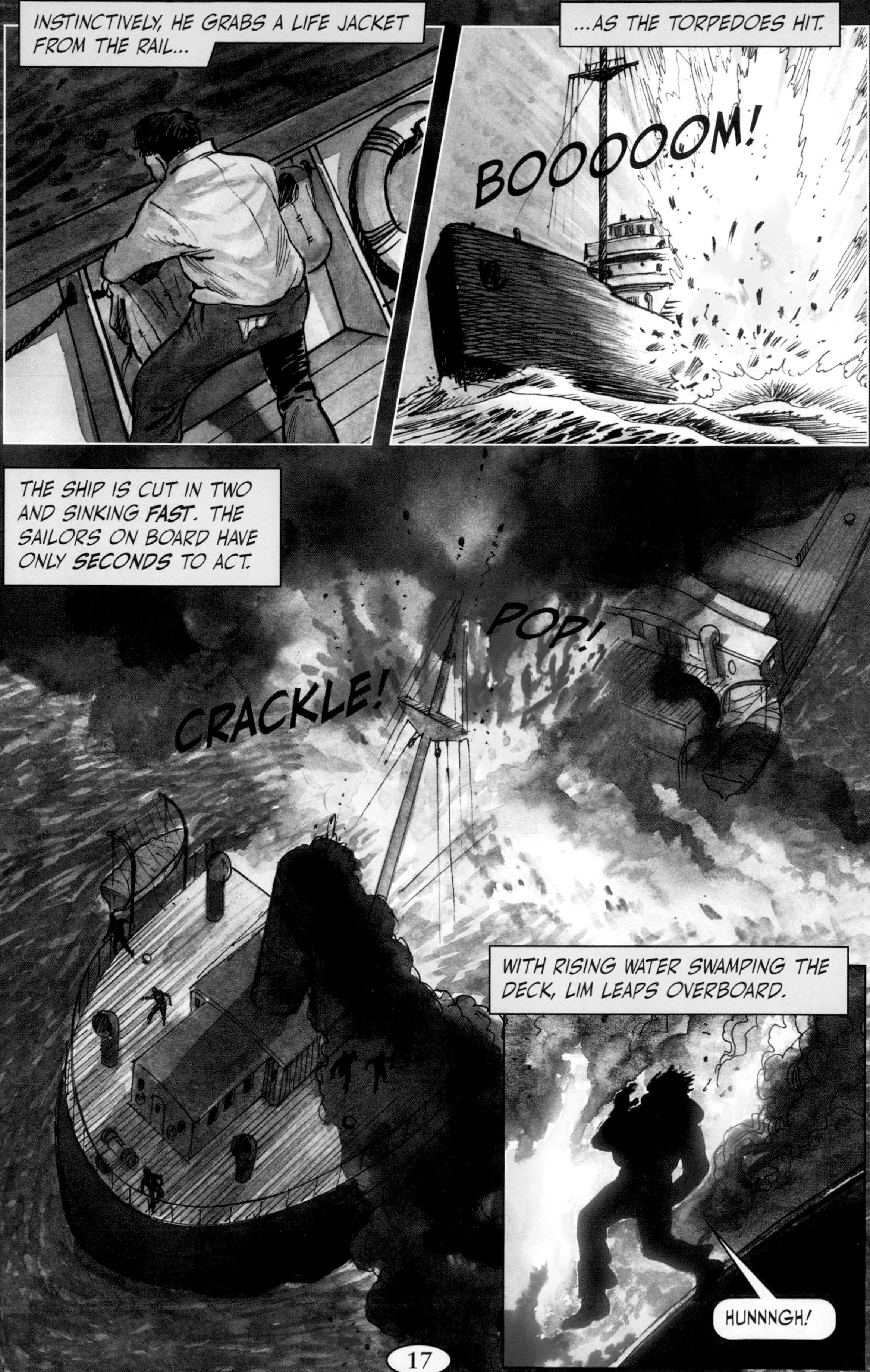
INSTINCTIVELY, HE GRABS A LIFE JACKET FROM THE RAIL...
...AS THE TORPEDOES HIT.
BOOOOOOM!
THE SHIP IS CUT IN TWO AND SINKING FAST. THE SAILORS ON BOARD HAVE ONLY SECONDS TO ACT.
POP!
CRACKLE!
WITH RISING WATER SWAMPING THE DECK, LIM LEAPS OVERBOARD.
HUNNNGH!

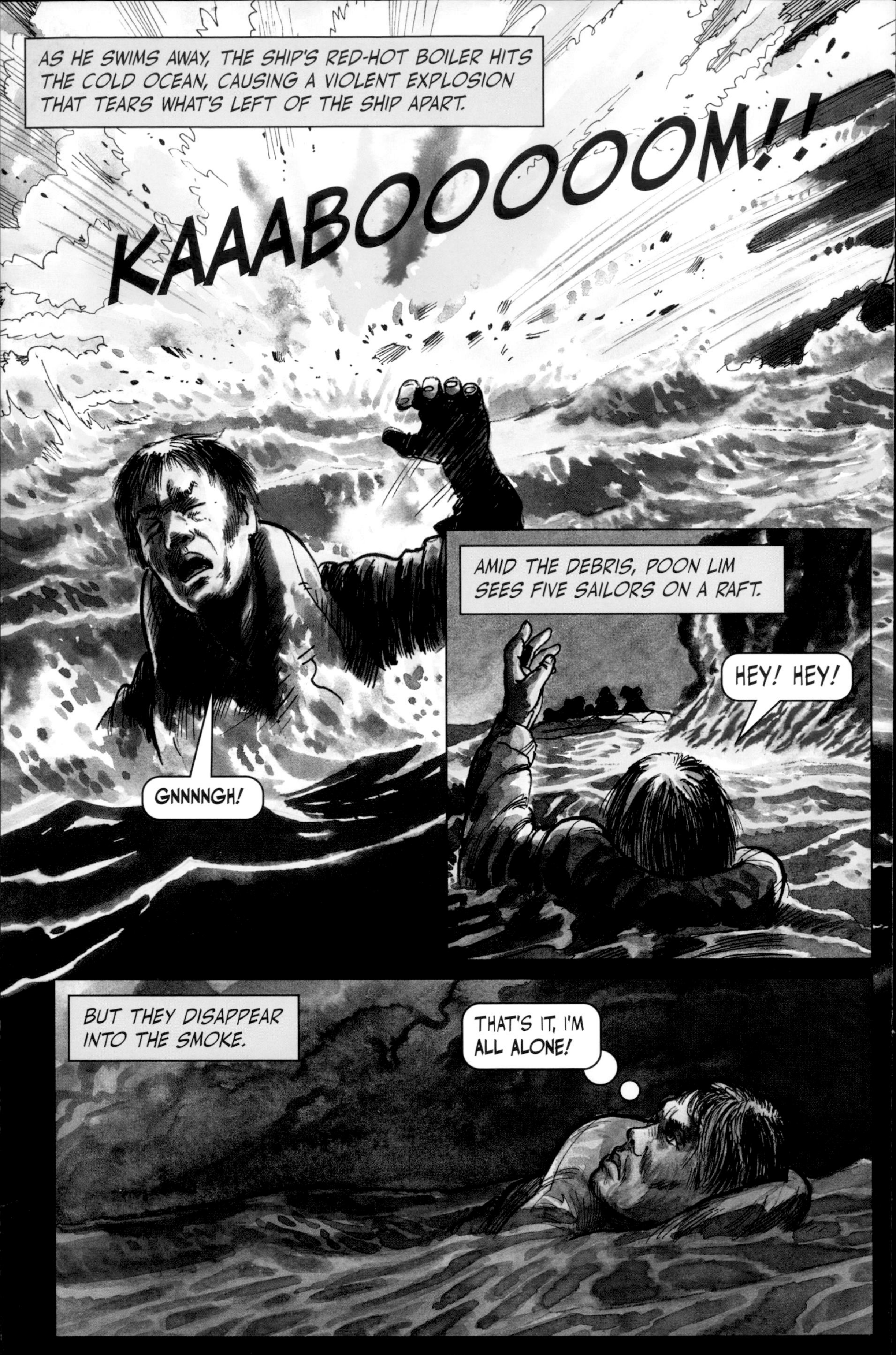
AS HE SWIMS AWAY, THE SHIP'S RED-HOT BOILER HITS THE COLD OCEAN, CAUSING A VIOLENT EXPLOSION THAT TEARS WHAT'S LEFT OF THE SHIP APART.
KAAABOOOOOM!!
GNNNNGH!
AMID THE DEBRIS, POON LIM SEES FIVE SAILORS ON A RAFT.
HEY! HEY!
BUT THEY DISAPPEAR INTO THE SMOKE.
THAT'S IT, I'M ALL ALONE!

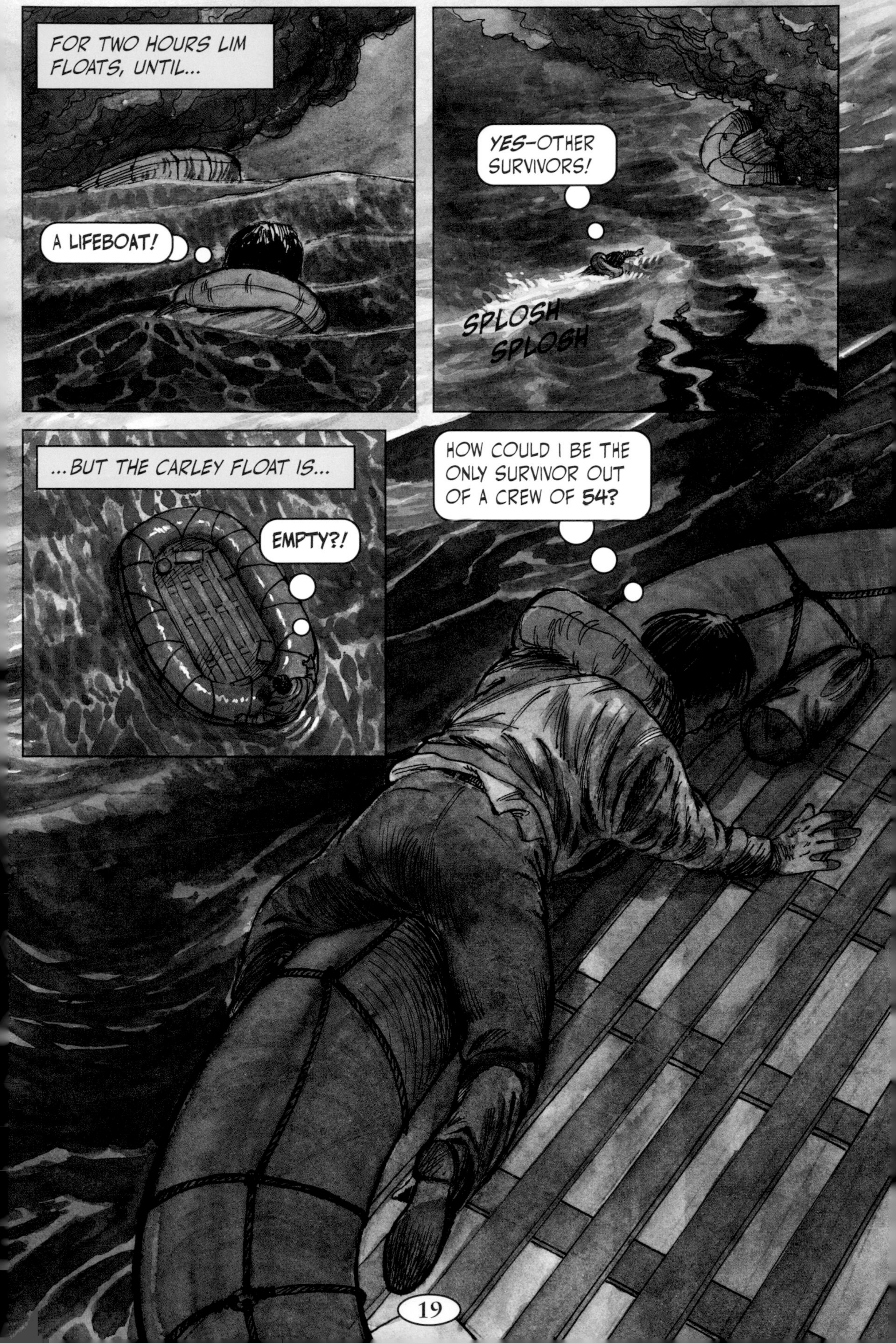
FOR TWO HOURS LIM FLOATS, UNTIL...
A LIFEBOAT!
YES—OTHER SURVIVORS!
SPLOSH SPLOSH
...BUT THE CARLEY FLOAT IS...
EMPTY?!
HOW COULD I BE THE ONLY SURVIVOR OUT OF A CREW OF 54?

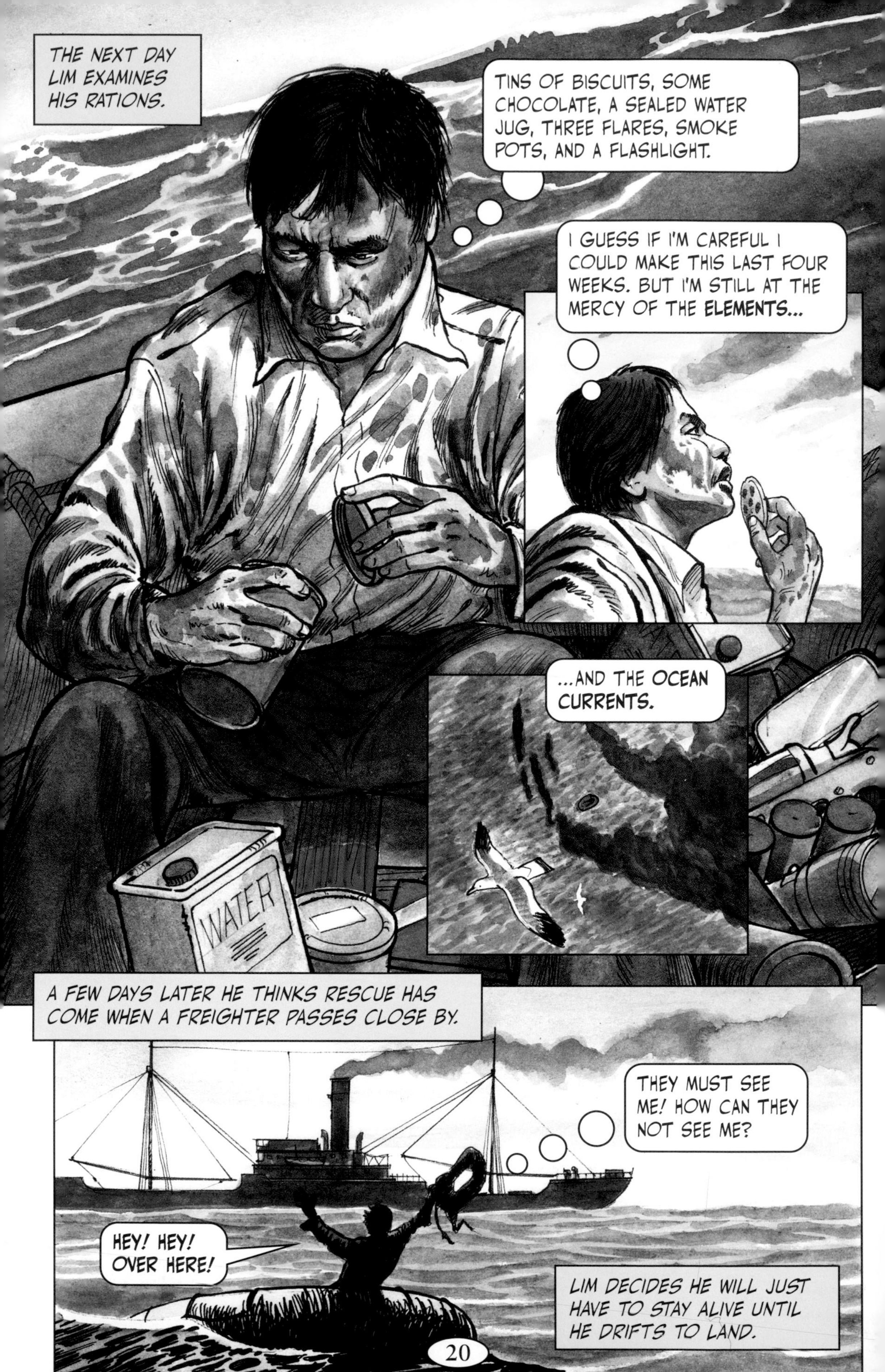
THE NEXT DAY LIM EXAMINES HIS RATIONS.
TINS OF BISCUITS, SOME CHOCOLATE, A SEALED WATER JUG, THREE FLARES, SMOKE POTS, AND A FLASHLIGHT.
I GUESS IF I'M CAREFUL I COULD MAKE THIS LAST FOUR WEEKS. BUT I'M STILL AT THE MERCY OF THE ELEMENTS...
...AND THE OCEAN CURRENTS.
WATER
A FEW DAYS LATER HE THINKS RESCUE HAS COME WHEN A FREIGHTER PASSES CLOSE BY.
THEY MUST SEE ME! HOW CAN THEY NOT SEE ME?
HEY! HEY! OVER HERE!
LIM DECIDES HE WILL JUST HAVE TO STAY ALIVE UNTIL HE DRIFTS TO LAND.

AFTER 28 DAYS THE FOOD AND WATER FROM THE RAFT HAVE RUN OUT, BUT BY ADAPTING THE LIFE BELT HE MAKES...

...A RAIN COLLECTOR!

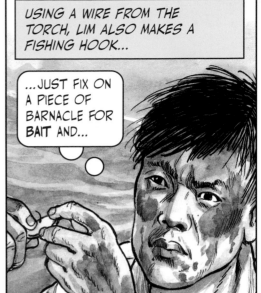

USING A WIRE FROM THE TORCH, LIM ALSO MAKES A FISHING HOOK...

...JUST FIX ON A PIECE OF BARNACLE FOR BAIT AND...

COME ON —BITE!

YES! I CAN GET WATER AND MEAT — I CAN SURVIVE!

HE EATS HALF THE FISH RAW AND USES THE OTHER HALF AS BAIT TO CATCH HIS NEXT FISH.

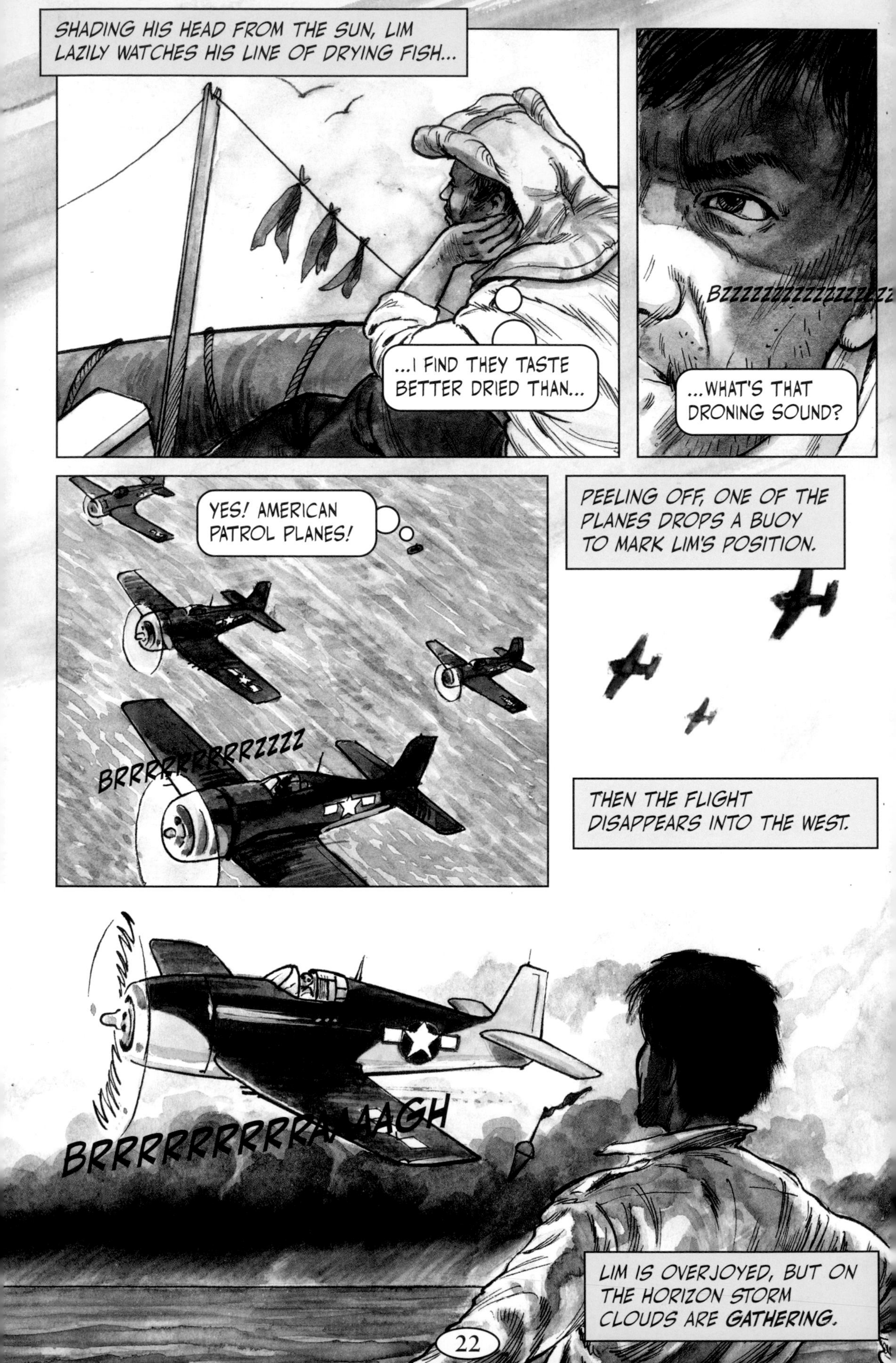
SHADING HIS HEAD FROM THE SUN, LIM LAZILY WATCHES HIS LINE OF DRYING FISH...
...I FIND THEY TASTE BETTER DRIED THAN...
BZZZZZZZZZZZZZZZZZ
...WHAT'S THAT DRONING SOUND?
YES! AMERICAN PATROL PLANES!
BRRRRRRRRRZZZZ
PEELING OFF, ONE OF THE PLANES DROPS A BUOY TO MARK LIM'S POSITION.
THEN THE FLIGHT DISAPPEARS INTO THE WEST.
BRRRRRRRRRAAAAGH
LIM IS OVERJOYED, BUT ON THE HORIZON STORM CLOUDS ARE GATHERING.

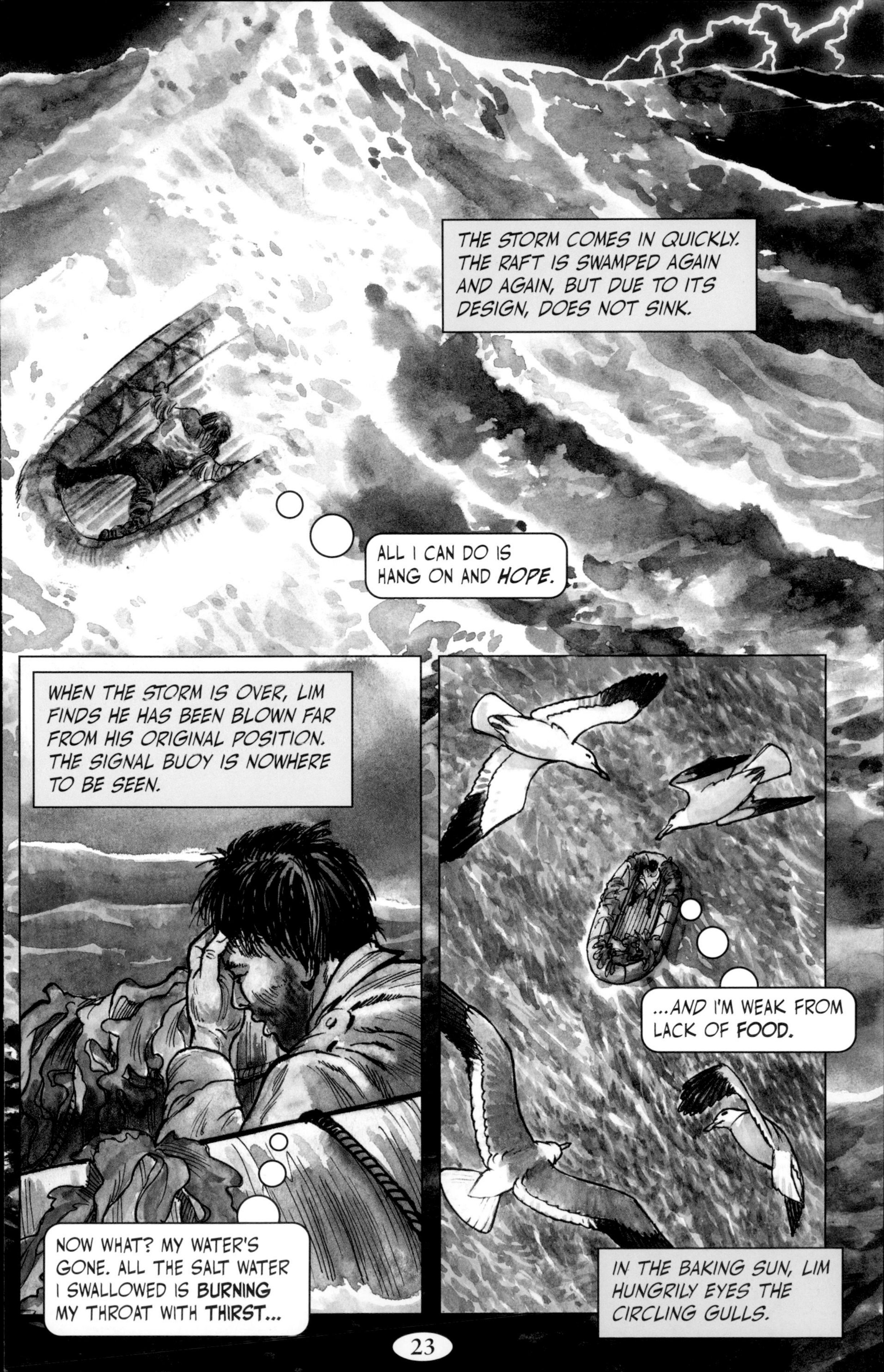
THE STORM COMES IN QUICKLY. THE RAFT IS SWAMPED AGAIN AND AGAIN, BUT DUE TO ITS DESIGN, DOES NOT SINK.
ALL I CAN DO IS HANG ON AND HOPE.
WHEN THE STORM IS OVER, LIM FINDS HE HAS BEEN BLOWN FAR FROM HIS ORIGINAL POSITION. THE SIGNAL BUOY IS NOWHERE TO BE SEEN.
NOW WHAT? MY WATER'S GONE. ALL THE SALT WATER I SWALLOWED IS BURNING MY THROAT WITH THIRST...
...AND I'M WEAK FROM LACK OF FOOD.
IN THE BAKING SUN, LIM HUNGRILY EYES THE CIRCLING GULLS.

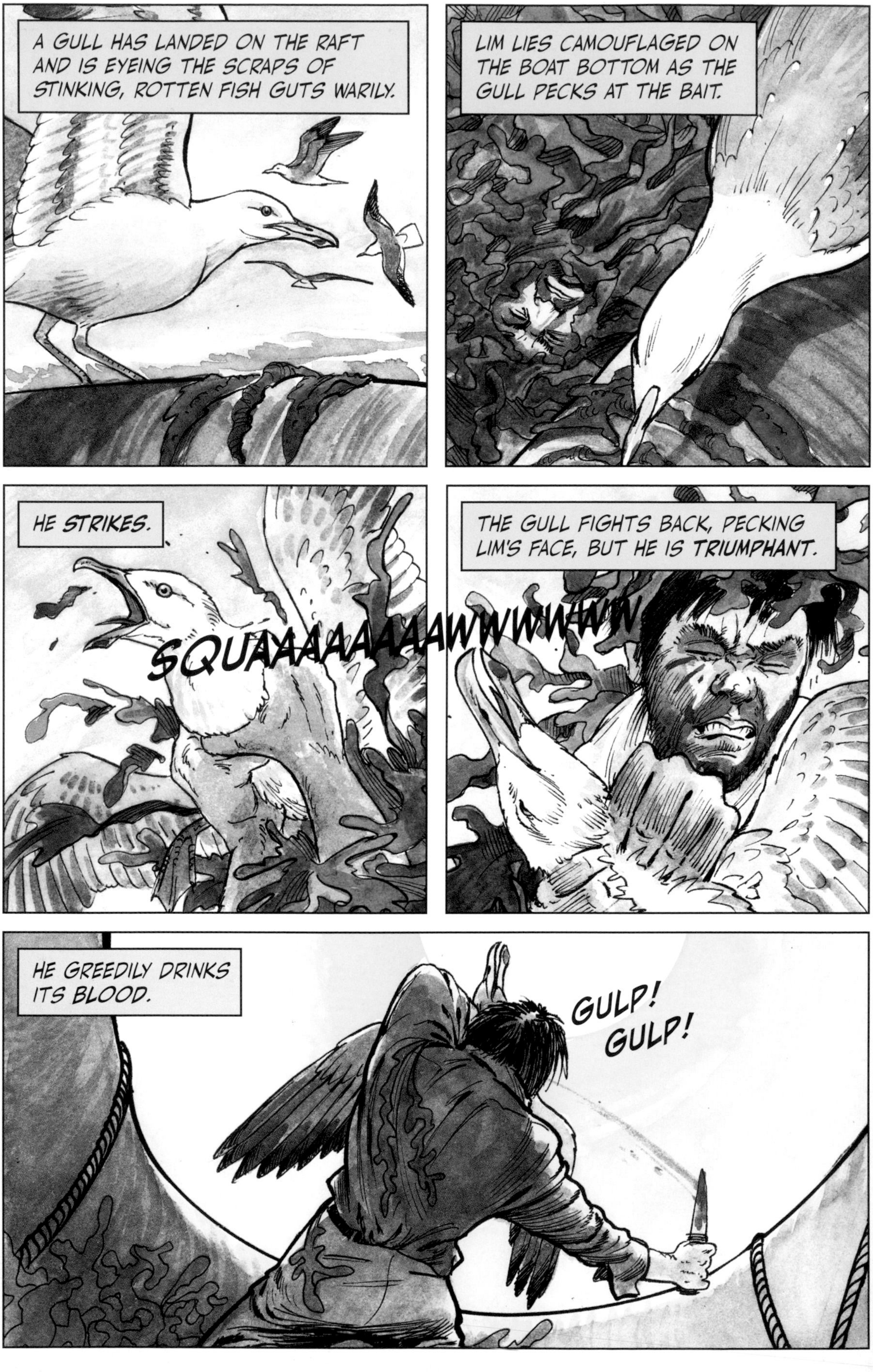
A GULL HAS LANDED ON THE RAFT AND IS EYEING THE SCRAPS OF STINKING, ROTTEN FISH GUTS WARILY.
LIM LIES CAMOUFLAGED ON THE BOAT BOTTOM AS THE GULL PECKS AT THE BAIT.
HE STRIKES.
SQUAAAAAAAAWWWWWWN
THE GULL FIGHTS BACK, PECKING LIM'S FACE, BUT HE IS TRIUMPHANT.
HE GREEDILY DRINKS ITS BLOOD.
GULP!
GULP!

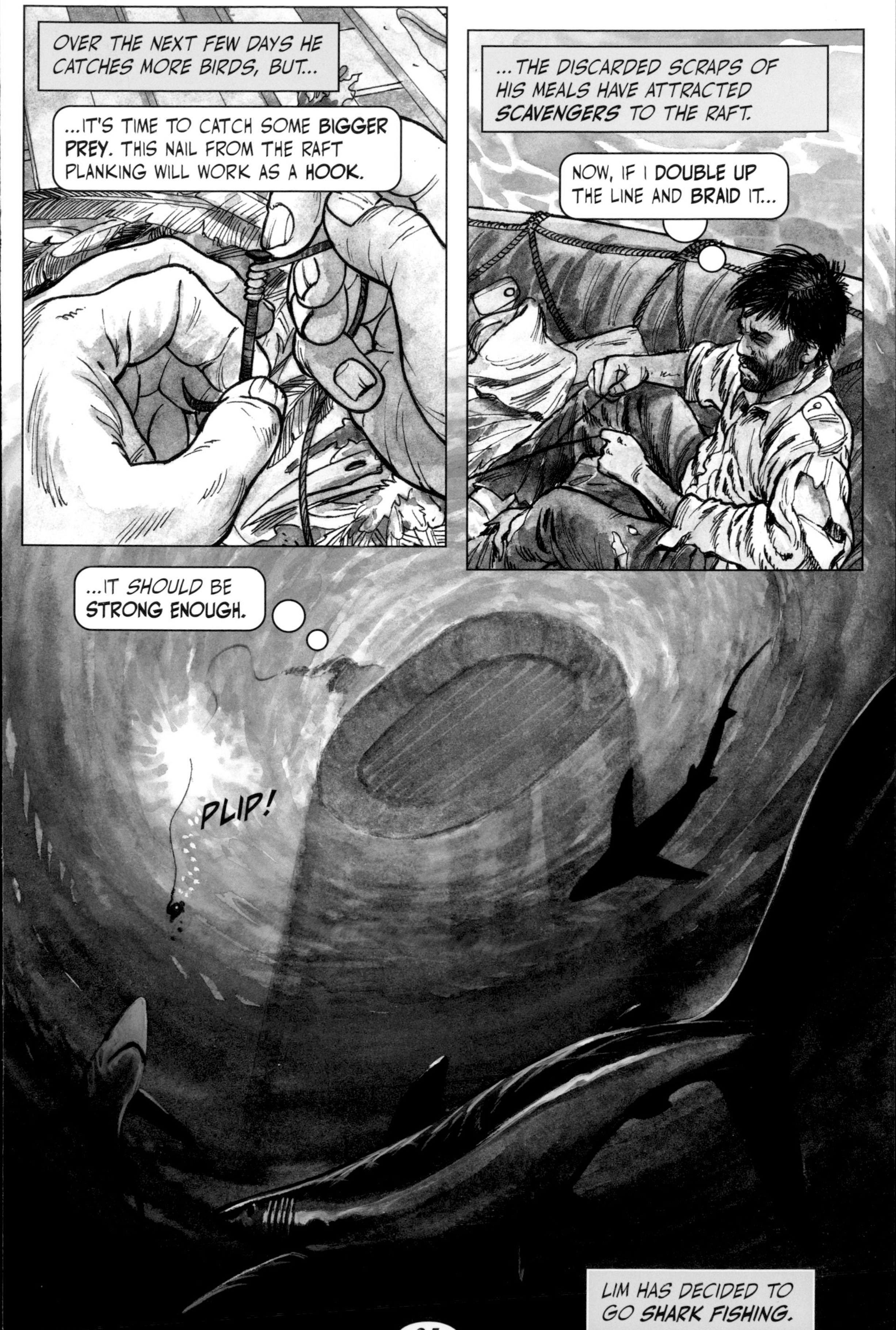
OVER THE NEXT FEW DAYS HE CATCHES MORE BIRDS, BUT...
...IT'S TIME TO CATCH SOME BIGGER PREY. THIS NAIL FROM THE RAFT PLANKING WILL WORK AS A HOOK.
...THE DISCARDED SCRAPS OF HIS MEALS HAVE ATTRACTED SCAVENGERS TO THE RAFT.
NOW, IF I DOUBLE UP THE LINE AND BRAID IT...
...IT SHOULD BE STRONG ENOUGH.
PLIP!
LIM HAS DECIDED TO GO SHARK FISHING.

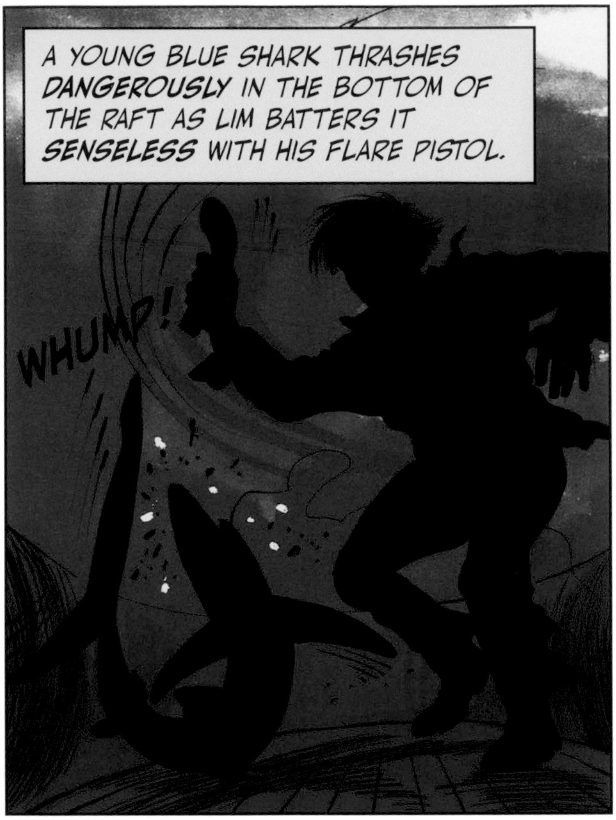
A YOUNG BLUE SHARK THRASHES DANGEROUSLY IN THE BOTTOM OF THE RAFT AS LIM BATTERS IT SENSELESS WITH HIS FLARE PISTOL.
WHUMP!

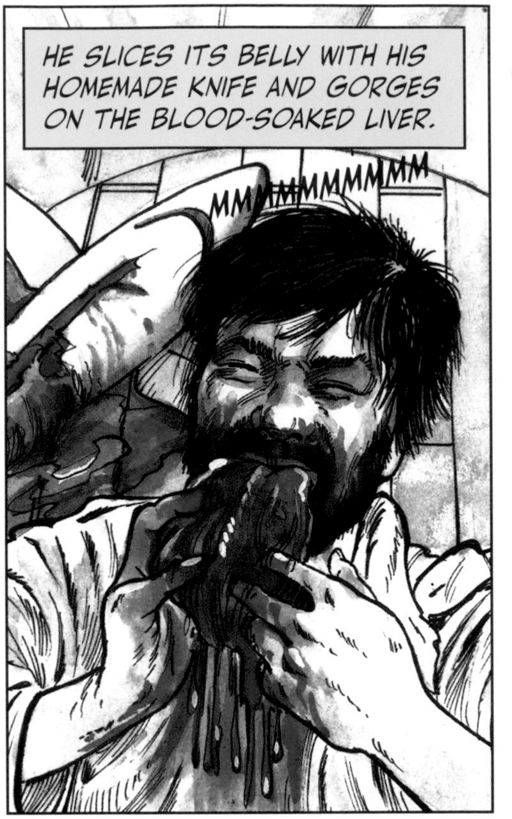
HE SLICES ITS BELLY WITH HIS HOMEMADE KNIFE AND GORGES ON THE BLOOD-SOAKED LIVER.
MMMMMMMMMMM

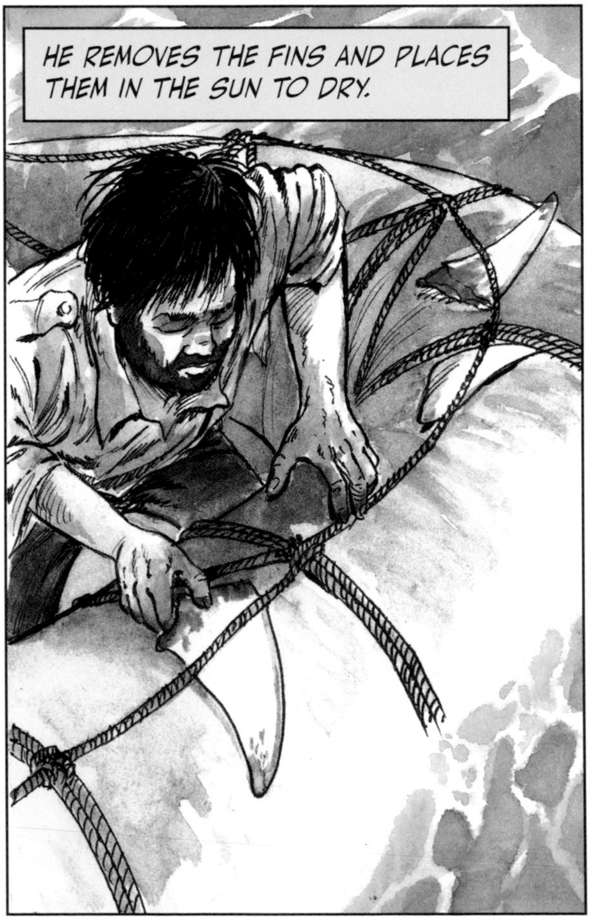
HE REMOVES THE FINS AND PLACES THEM IN THE SUN TO DRY.

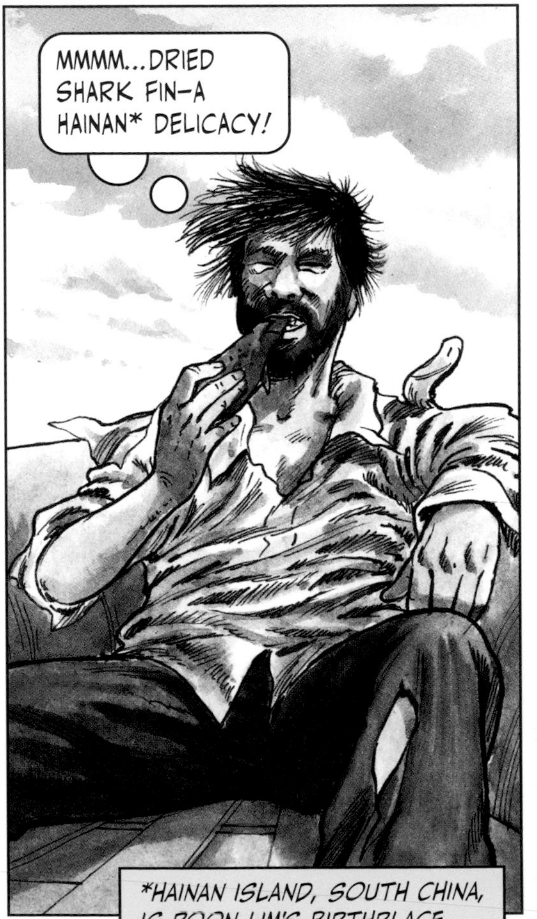
MMMM...DRIED SHARK FIN–A HAINAN* DELICACY!
*HAINAN ISLAND, SOUTH CHINA, IS POON LIM'S BIRTHPLACE.

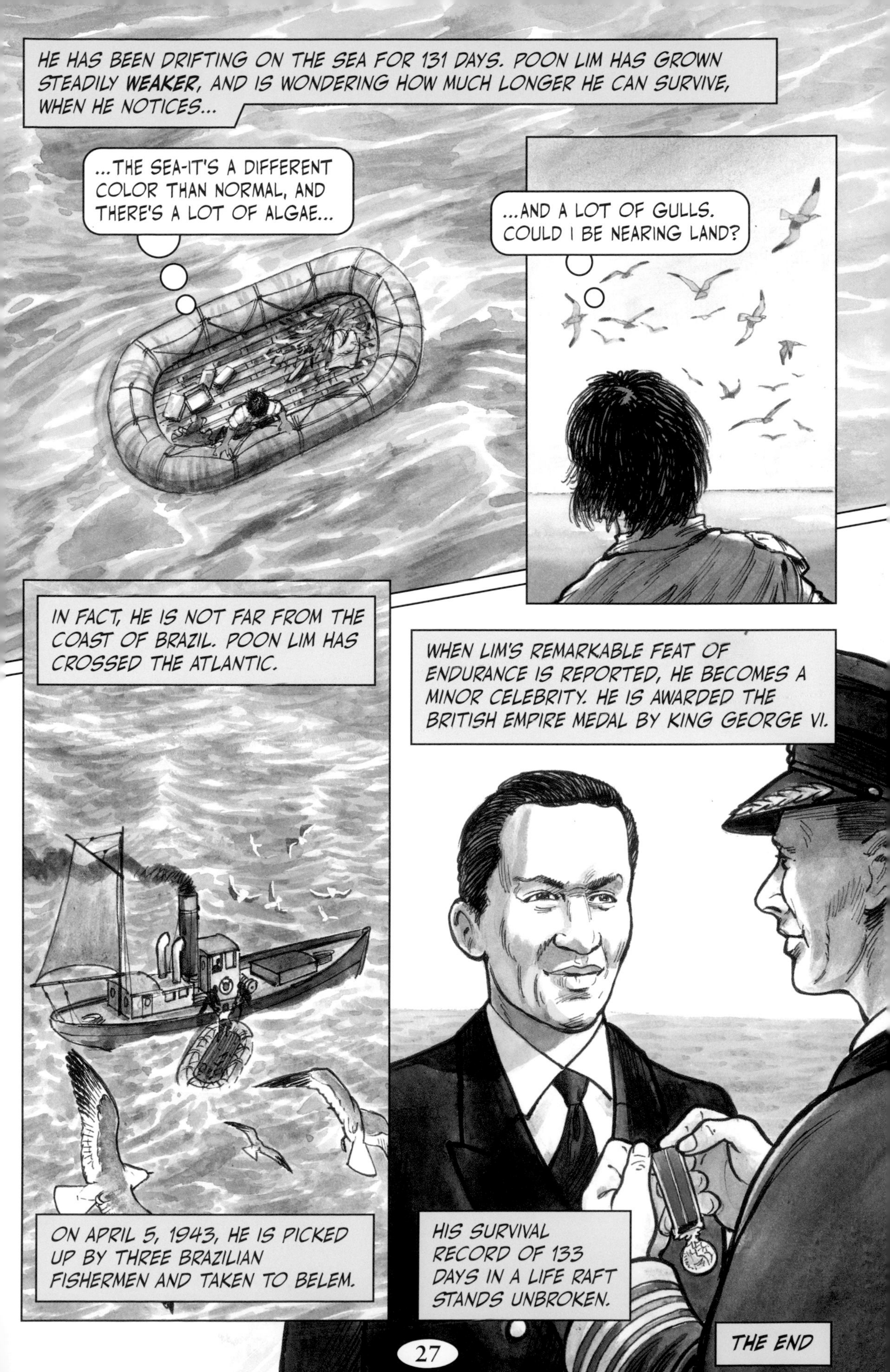
HE HAS BEEN DRIFTING ON THE SEA FOR 131 DAYS. POON LIM HAS GROWN STEADILY WEAKER, AND IS WONDERING HOW MUCH LONGER HE CAN SURVIVE, WHEN HE NOTICES...
...THE SEA-IT'S A DIFFERENT COLOR THAN NORMAL, AND THERE'S A LOT OF ALGAE...
...AND A LOT OF GULLS. COULD I BE NEARING LAND?
IN FACT, HE IS NOT FAR FROM THE COAST OF BRAZIL. POON LIM HAS CROSSED THE ATLANTIC.
ON APRIL 5, 1943, HE IS PICKED UP BY THREE BRAZILIAN FISHERMEN AND TAKEN TO BELEM.
WHEN LIM'S REMARKABLE FEAT OF ENDURANCE IS REPORTED, HE BECOMES A MINOR CELEBRITY. HE IS AWARDED THE BRITISH EMPIRE MEDAL BY KING GEORGE VI.
HIS SURVIVAL RECORD OF 133 DAYS IN A LIFE RAFT STANDS UNBROKEN.
THE END

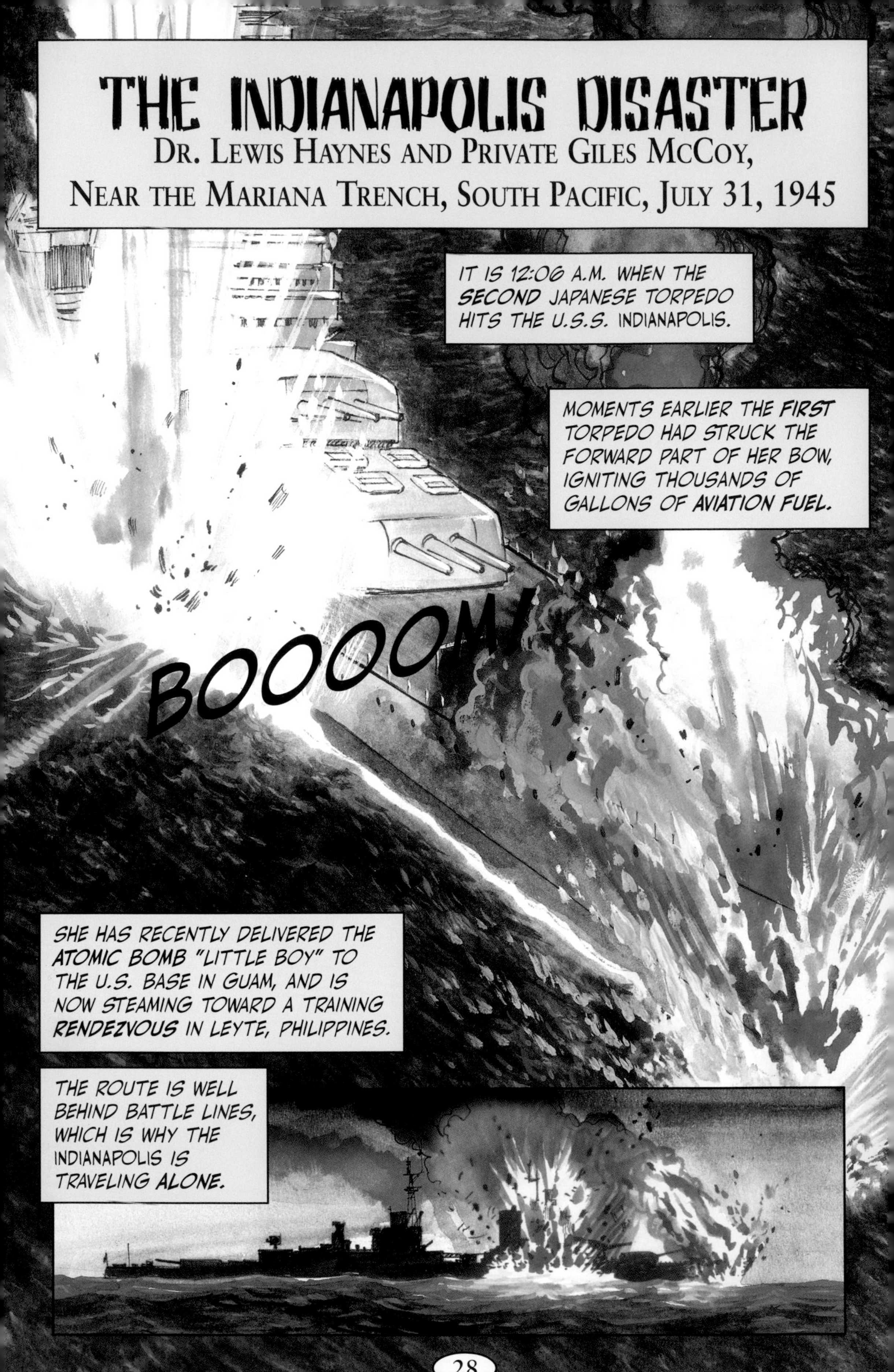
THE INDIANAPOLIS DISASTER
DR. LEWIS HAYNES AND PRIVATE GILES MCCOY,
NEAR THE MARIANA TRENCH, SOUTH PACIFIC, JULY 31, 1945
IT IS 12:06 A.M. WHEN THE SECOND JAPANESE TORPEDO HITS THE U.S.S. INDIANAPOLIS.
MOMENTS EARLIER THE FIRST TORPEDO HAD STRUCK THE FORWARD PART OF HER BOW, IGNITING THOUSANDS OF GALLONS OF AVIATION FUEL.
BOOOOOM!
SHE HAS RECENTLY DELIVERED THE ATOMIC BOMB "LITTLE BOY" TO THE U.S. BASE IN GUAM, AND IS NOW STEAMING TOWARD A TRAINING RENDEZVOUS IN LEYTE, PHILIPPINES.
THE ROUTE IS WELL BEHIND BATTLE LINES, WHICH IS WHY THE INDIANAPOLIS IS TRAVELING ALONE.

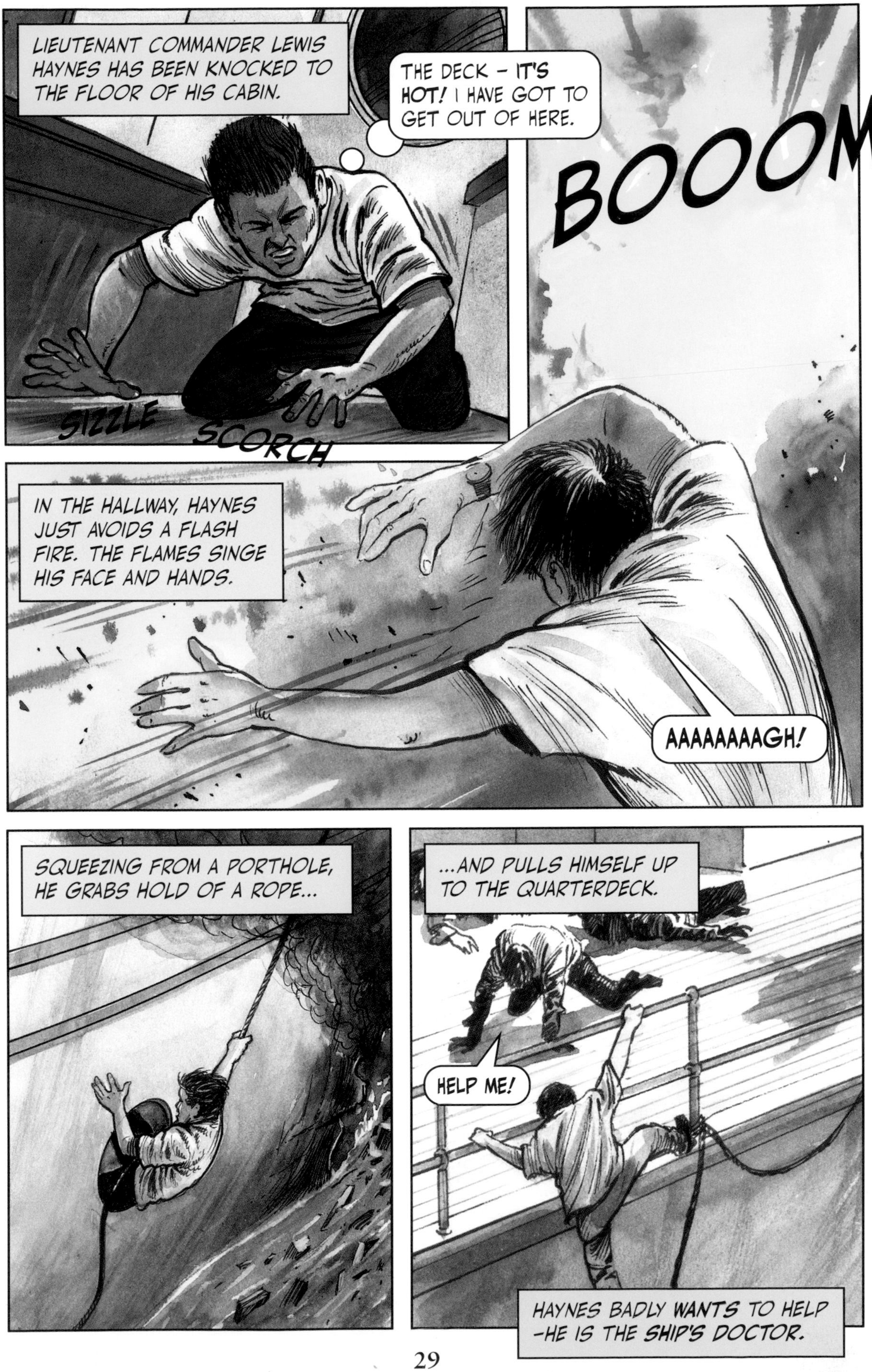

LIEUTENANT COMMANDER LEWIS HAYNES HAS BEEN KNOCKED TO THE FLOOR OF HIS CABIN.
THE DECK – IT'S HOT! I HAVE GOT TO GET OUT OF HERE.
SIZZLE
SCORCH
BOOOM
IN THE HALLWAY, HAYNES JUST AVOIDS A FLASH FIRE. THE FLAMES SINGE HIS FACE AND HANDS.
AAAAAAAAGH!
SQUEEZING FROM A PORTHOLE, HE GRABS HOLD OF A ROPE...
...AND PULLS HIMSELF UP TO THE QUARTERDECK.
HELP ME!
HAYNES BADLY WANTS TO HELP –HE IS THE SHIP'S DOCTOR.

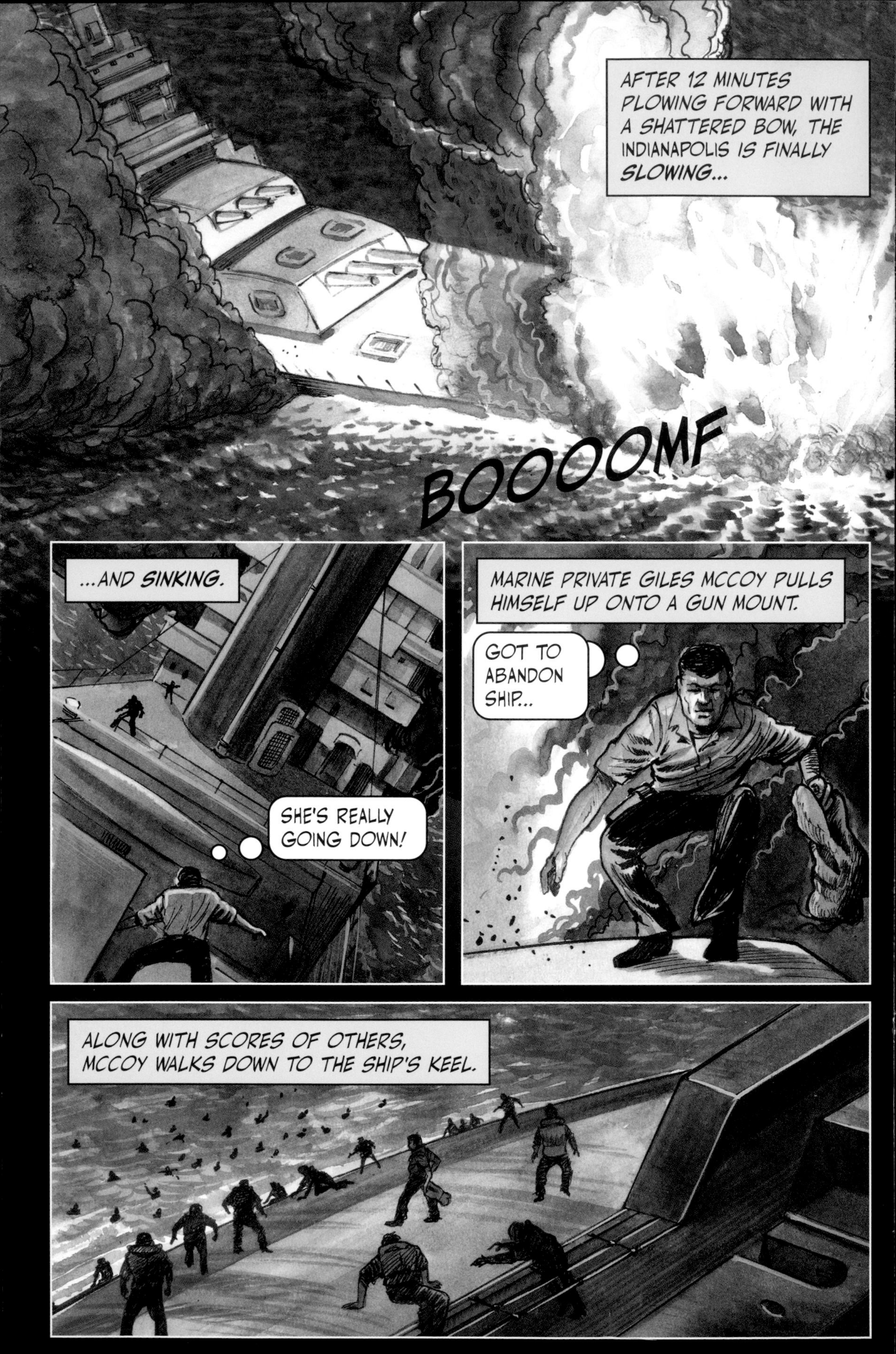
AFTER 12 MINUTES PLOWING FORWARD WITH A SHATTERED BOW, THE INDIANAPOLIS IS FINALLY SLOWING...
BOOOOOMF
...AND SINKING.
SHE'S REALLY GOING DOWN!
MARINE PRIVATE GILES MCCOY PULLS HIMSELF UP ONTO A GUN MOUNT.
GOT TO ABANDON SHIP...
ALONG WITH SCORES OF OTHERS, MCCOY WALKS DOWN TO THE SHIP'S KEEL.

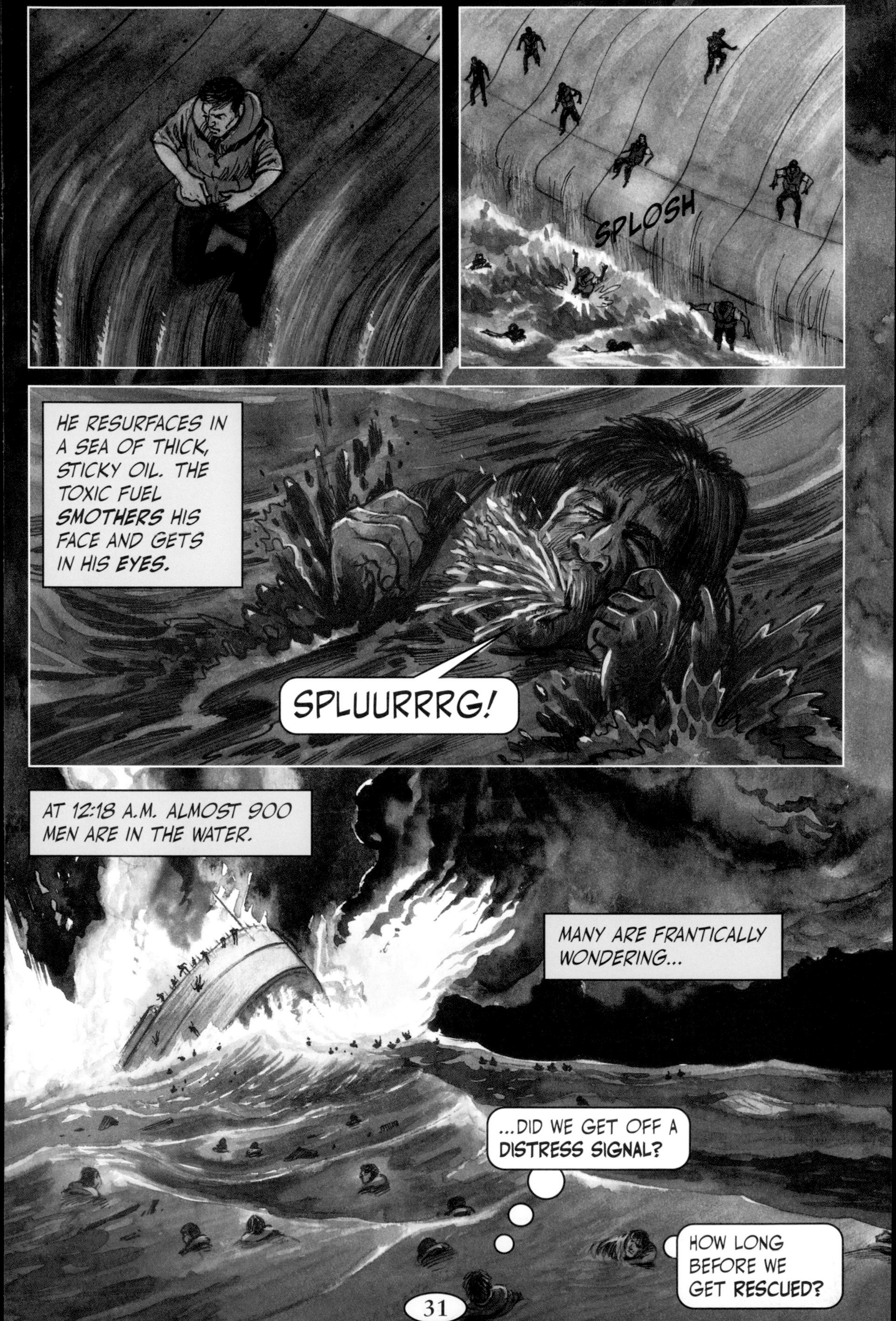
SPLOSH
HE RESURFACES IN A SEA OF THICK, STICKY OIL. THE TOXIC FUEL SMOTHERS HIS FACE AND GETS IN HIS EYES.
SPLUURRRG!
AT 12:18 A.M. ALMOST 900 MEN ARE IN THE WATER.
MANY ARE FRANTICALLY WONDERING...
...DID WE GET OFF A DISTRESS SIGNAL?
HOW LONG BEFORE WE GET RESCUED?

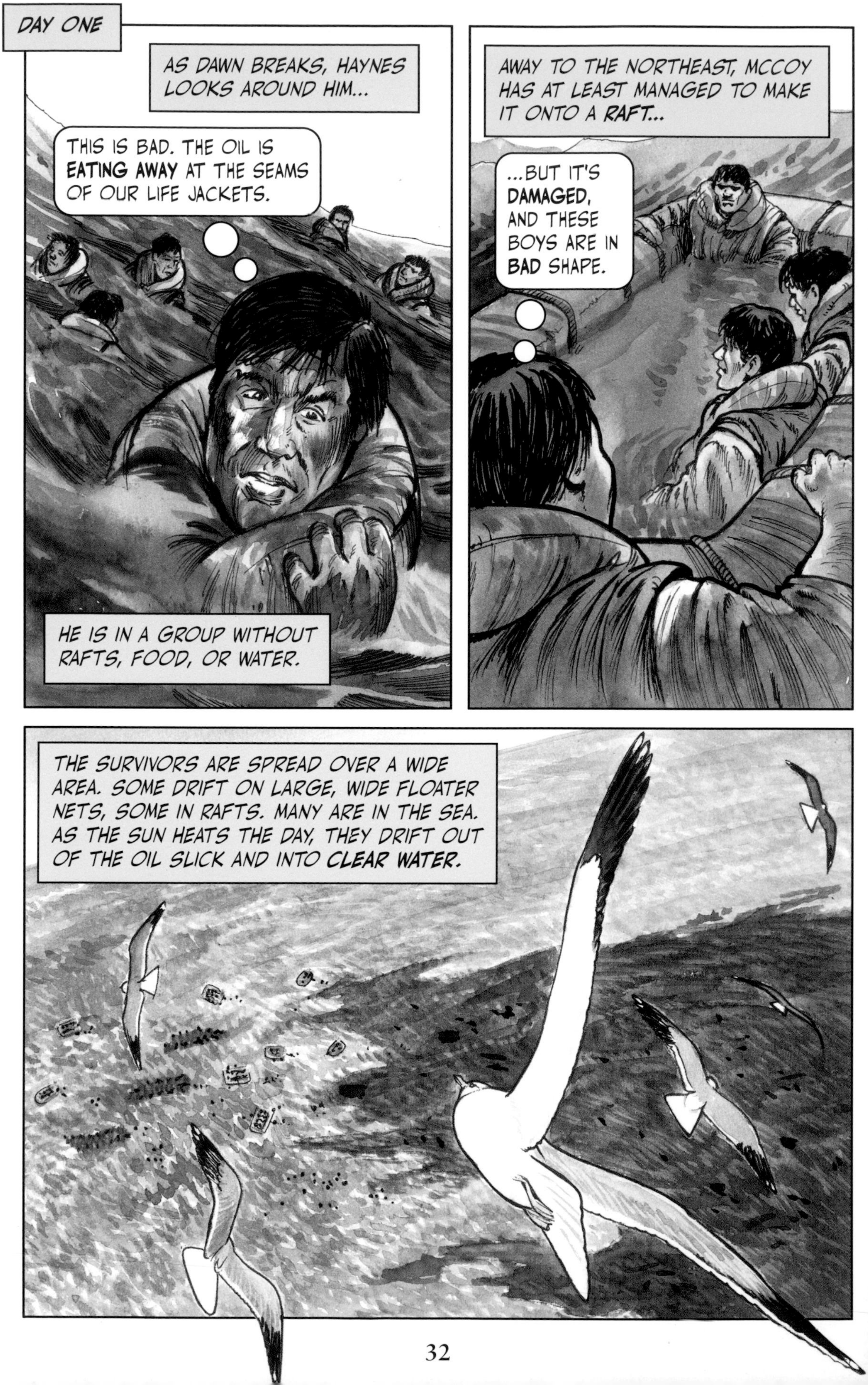
DAY ONE
AS DAWN BREAKS, HAYNES LOOKS AROUND HIM...
THIS IS BAD. THE OIL IS EATING AWAY AT THE SEAMS OF OUR LIFE JACKETS.
HE IS IN A GROUP WITHOUT RAFTS, FOOD, OR WATER.
AWAY TO THE NORTHEAST, MCCOY HAS AT LEAST MANAGED TO MAKE IT ONTO A RAFT...
...BUT IT'S DAMAGED, AND THESE BOYS ARE IN BAD SHAPE.
THE SURVIVORS ARE SPREAD OVER A WIDE AREA. SOME DRIFT ON LARGE, WIDE FLOATER NETS, SOME IN RAFTS. MANY ARE IN THE SEA. AS THE SUN HEATS THE DAY, THEY DRIFT OUT OF THE OIL SLICK AND INTO CLEAR WATER.

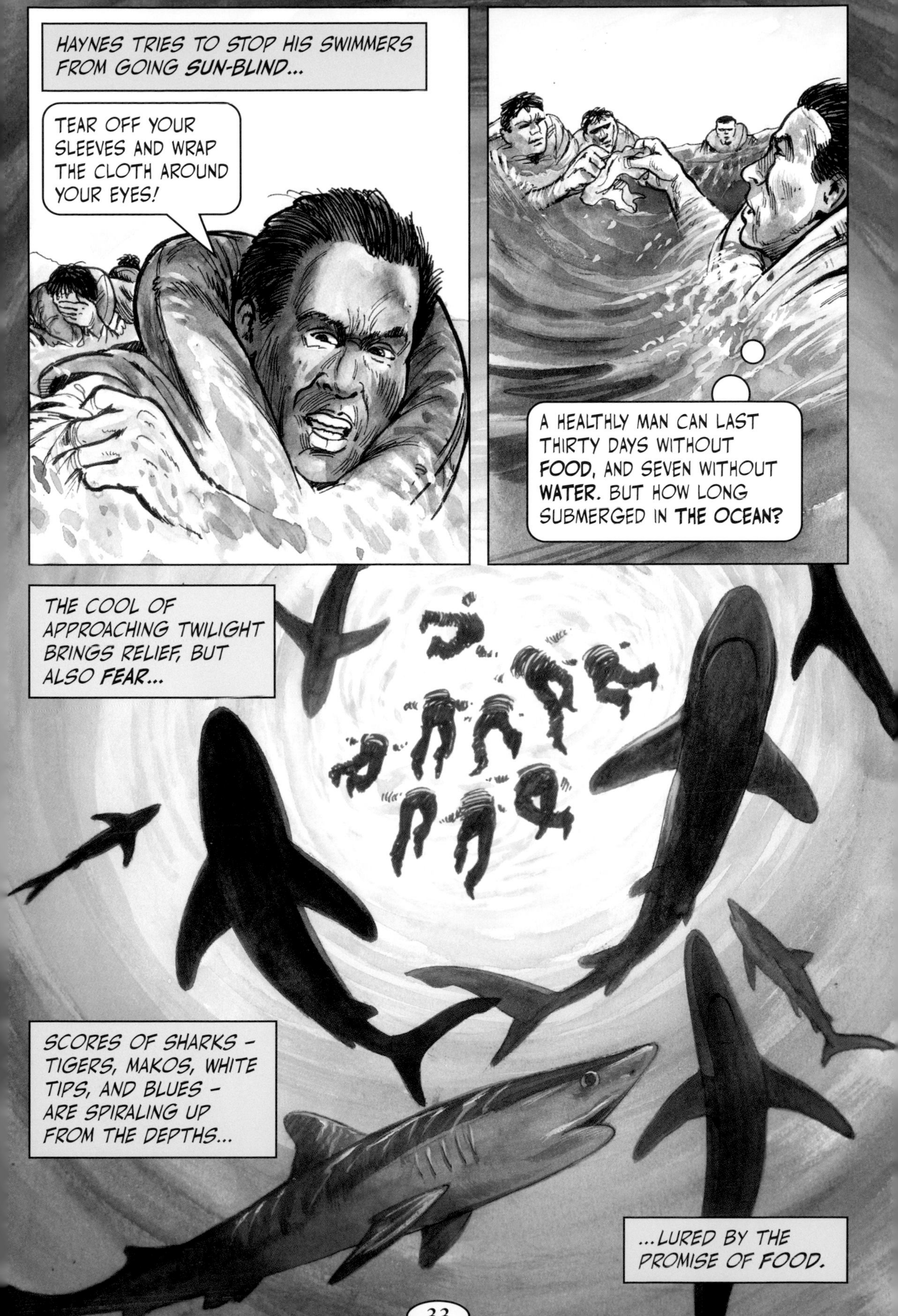
HAYNES TRIES TO STOP HIS SWIMMERS FROM GOING SUN-BLIND...
TEAR OFF YOUR SLEEVES AND WRAP THE CLOTH AROUND YOUR EYES!
A HEALTHLY MAN CAN LAST THIRTY DAYS WITHOUT FOOD, AND SEVEN WITHOUT WATER. BUT HOW LONG SUBMERGED IN THE OCEAN?
THE COOL OF APPROACHING TWILIGHT BRINGS RELIEF, BUT ALSO FEAR...
SCORES OF SHARKS - TIGERS, MAKOS, WHITE TIPS, AND BLUES - ARE SPIRALING UP FROM THE DEPTHS...
...LURED BY THE PROMISE OF FOOD.

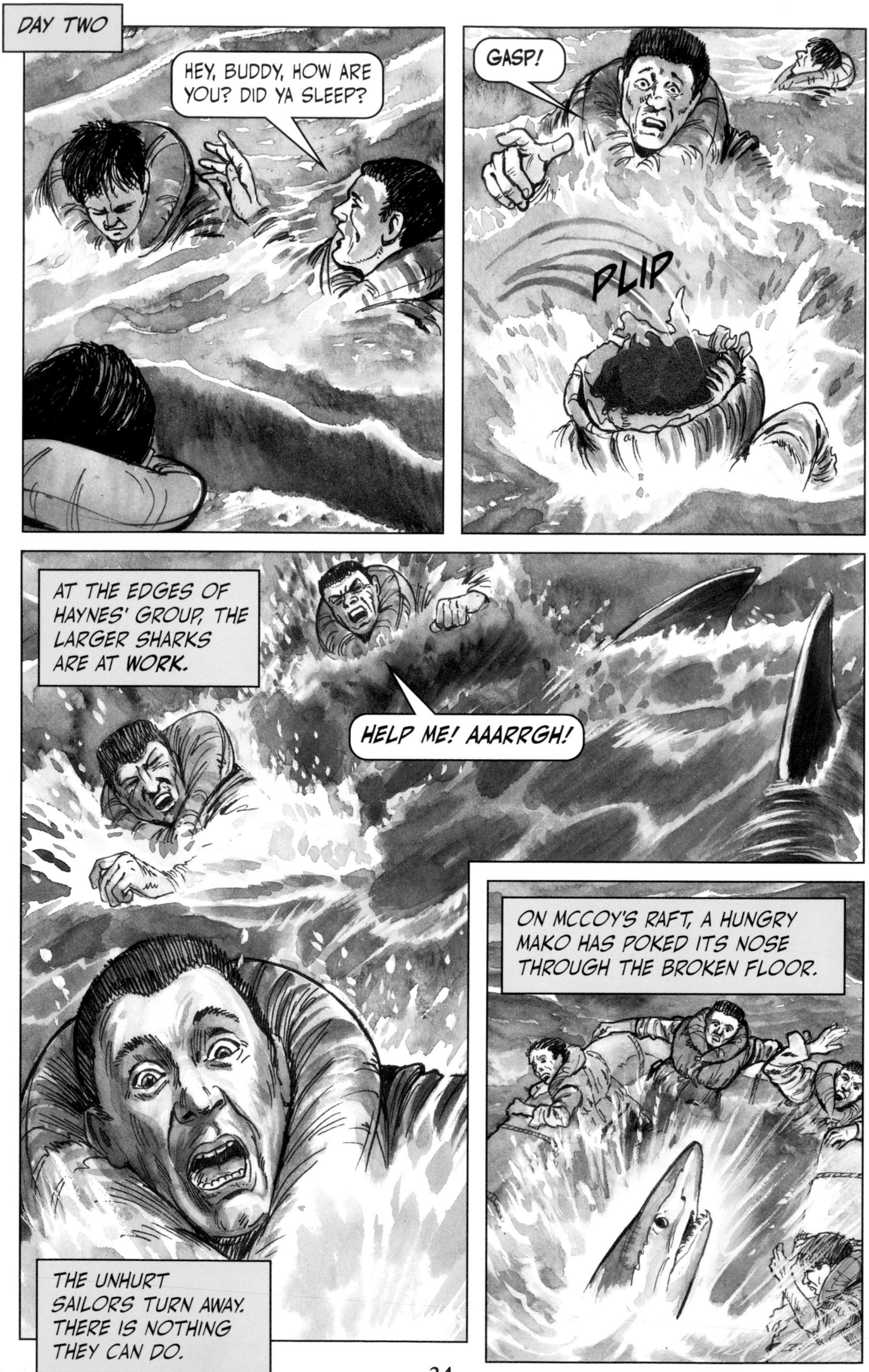
DAY TWO
HEY, BUDDY, HOW ARE YOU? DID YA SLEEP?
GASP!
PLIP
AT THE EDGES OF HAYNES' GROUP, THE LARGER SHARKS ARE AT WORK.
HELP ME! AAARRGH!
THE UNHURT SAILORS TURN AWAY. THERE IS NOTHING THEY CAN DO.
ON MCCOY'S RAFT, A HUNGRY MAKO HAS POKED ITS NOSE THROUGH THE BROKEN FLOOR.

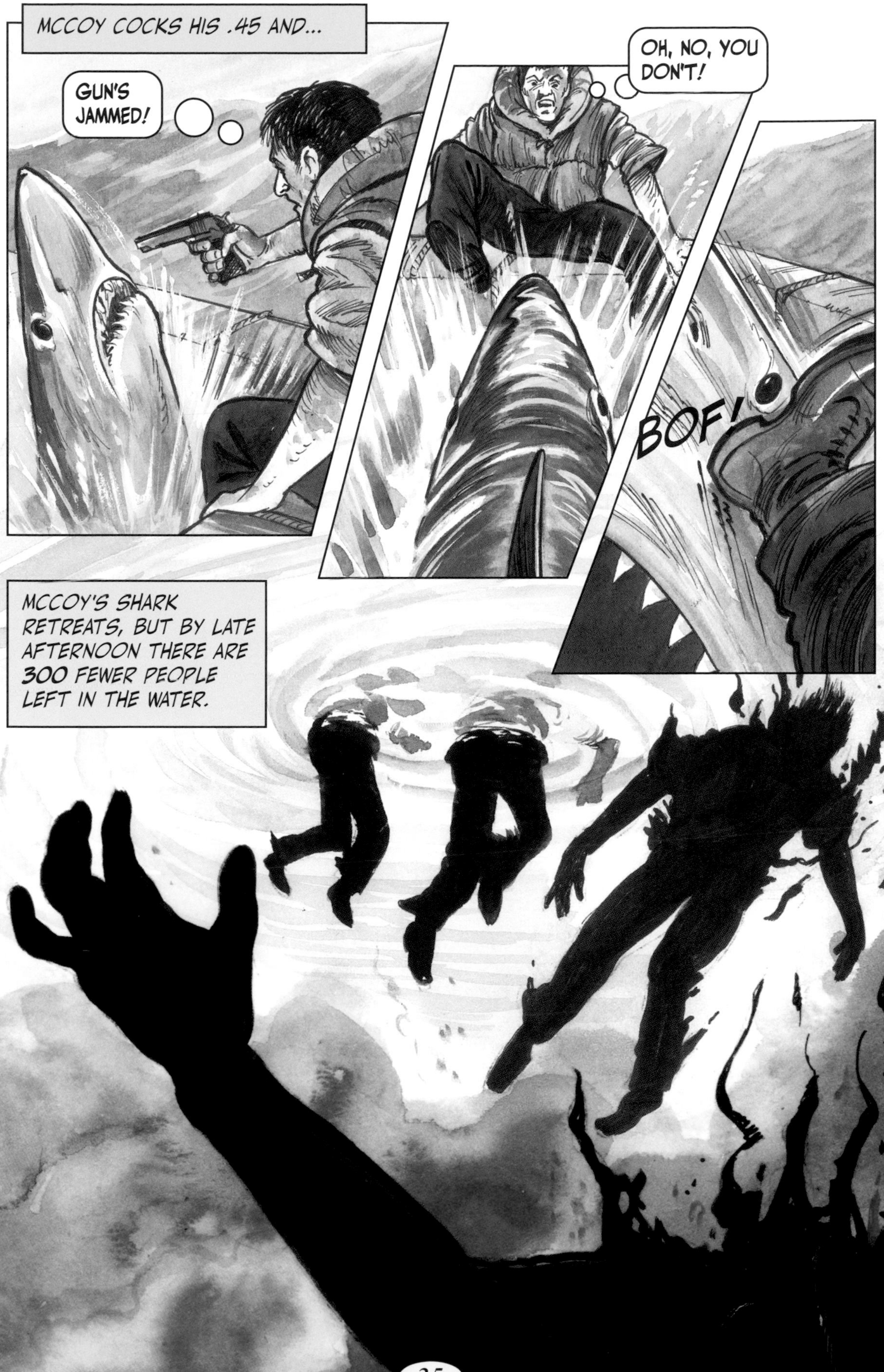
MCCOY COCKS HIS .45 AND...
GUN'S JAMMED!
OH, NO, YOU DON'T!
BOF!
MCCOY'S SHARK RETREATS, BUT BY LATE AFTERNOON THERE ARE 300 FEWER PEOPLE LEFT IN THE WATER.

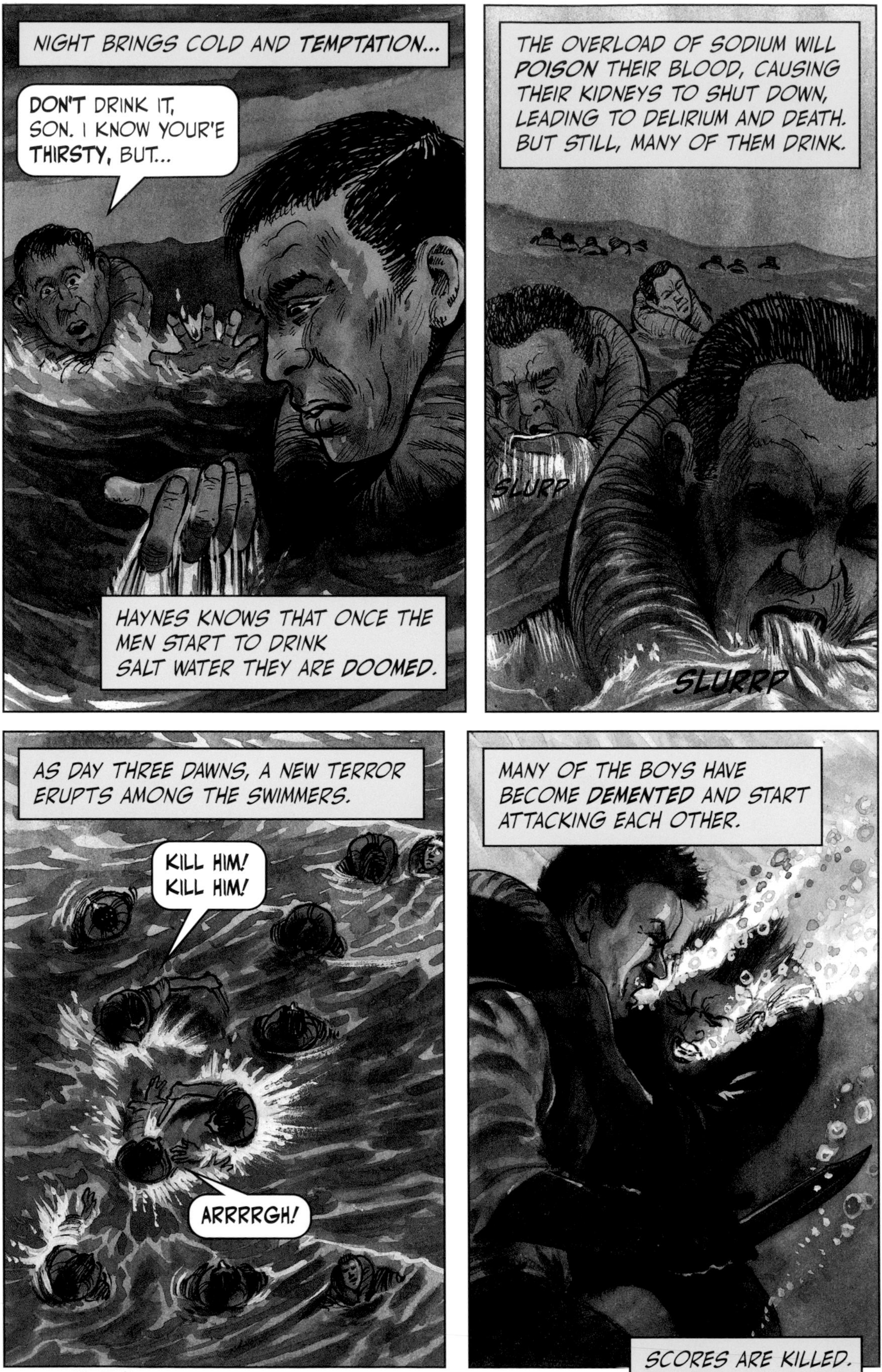
NIGHT BRINGS COLD AND TEMPTATION...
DON'T DRINK IT, SON. I KNOW YOUR'E THIRSTY, BUT...
HAYNES KNOWS THAT ONCE THE MEN START TO DRINK SALT WATER THEY ARE DOOMED.
THE OVERLOAD OF SODIUM WILL POISON THEIR BLOOD, CAUSING THEIR KIDNEYS TO SHUT DOWN, LEADING TO DELIRIUM AND DEATH. BUT STILL, MANY OF THEM DRINK.
SLURP
SLURRP
AS DAY THREE DAWNS, A NEW TERROR ERUPTS AMONG THE SWIMMERS.
KILL HIM! KILL HIM!
ARRRRGH!
MANY OF THE BOYS HAVE BECOME DEMENTED AND START ATTACKING EACH OTHER.
SCORES ARE KILLED.

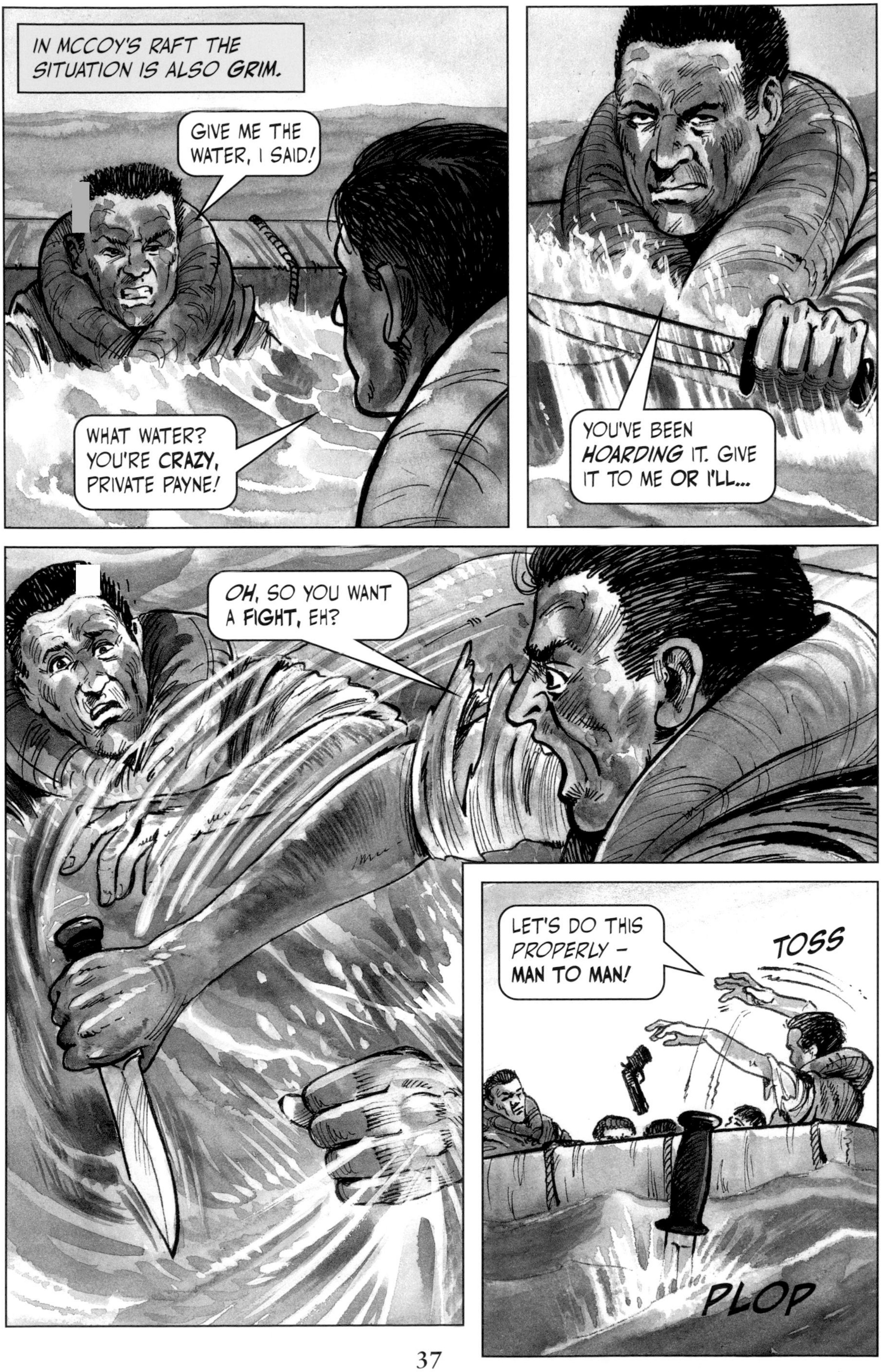
IN MCCOY'S RAFT THE SITUATION IS ALSO GRIM.
GIVE ME THE WATER, I SAID!
WHAT WATER? YOU'RE CRAZY, PRIVATE PAYNE!
YOU'VE BEEN HOARDING IT. GIVE IT TO ME OR I'LL...
OH, SO YOU WANT A FIGHT, EH?
LET'S DO THIS PROPERLY – MAN TO MAN!
TOSS
PLOP

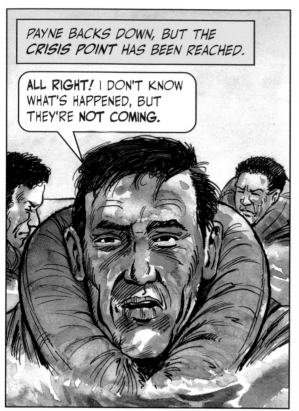

PAYNE BACKS DOWN, BUT THE **CRISIS POINT** HAS BEEN REACHED.

ALL RIGHT! I DON'T KNOW WHAT'S HAPPENED, BUT THEY'RE **NOT COMING.**

WE MIGHT AS WELL FACE IT — WE'RE ALL GOING TO **DIE** IN THIS OCEAN.

STRANGELY, MCCOY FEELS BETTER NOW THAT HE HAS SAID IT. NOW HE NO LONGER HAS TO LIVE ON **FALSE HOPE.**

DAY FOUR, AND HAYNES' SWIMMERS HAVE BEEN SUBMERGED FOR OVER **70 HOURS.**

MOST OF THEM ARE BARELY AFLOAT.

THE **CAUSTIC** SALT WATER HAS EATEN HOLES IN THEIR SKIN.

DEHYDRATED AND STARVING, THEY ARE FINDING IT HARD TO **WANT** TO STAY ALIVE.

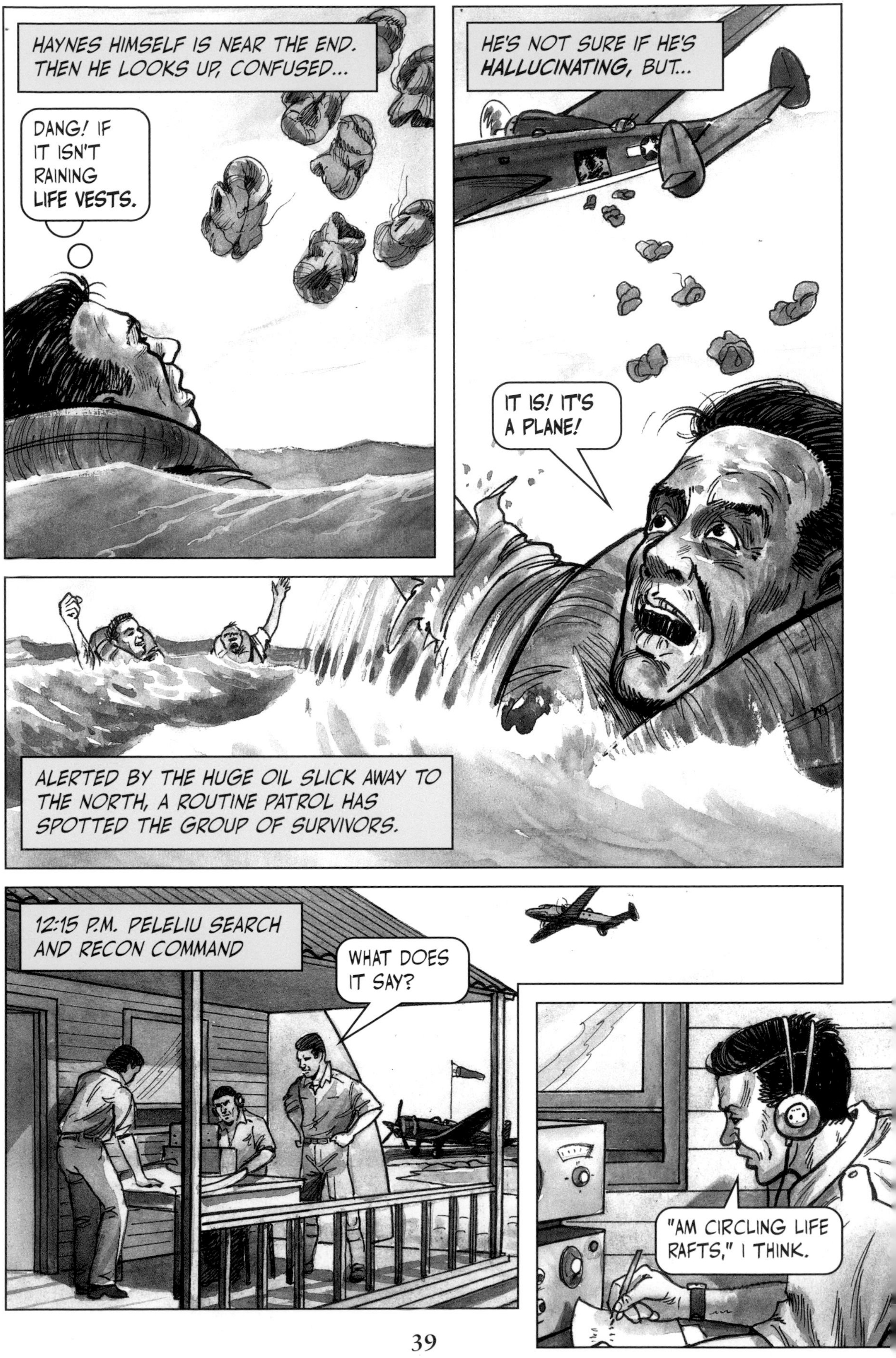
HAYNES HIMSELF IS NEAR THE END. THEN HE LOOKS UP, CONFUSED...
DANG! IF IT ISN'T RAINING LIFE VESTS.
HE'S NOT SURE IF HE'S HALLUCINATING, BUT...
IT IS! IT'S A PLANE!
ALERTED BY THE HUGE OIL SLICK AWAY TO THE NORTH, A ROUTINE PATROL HAS SPOTTED THE GROUP OF SURVIVORS.
12:15 P.M. PELELIU SEARCH AND RECON COMMAND
WHAT DOES IT SAY?
"AM CIRCLING LIFE RAFTS," I THINK.

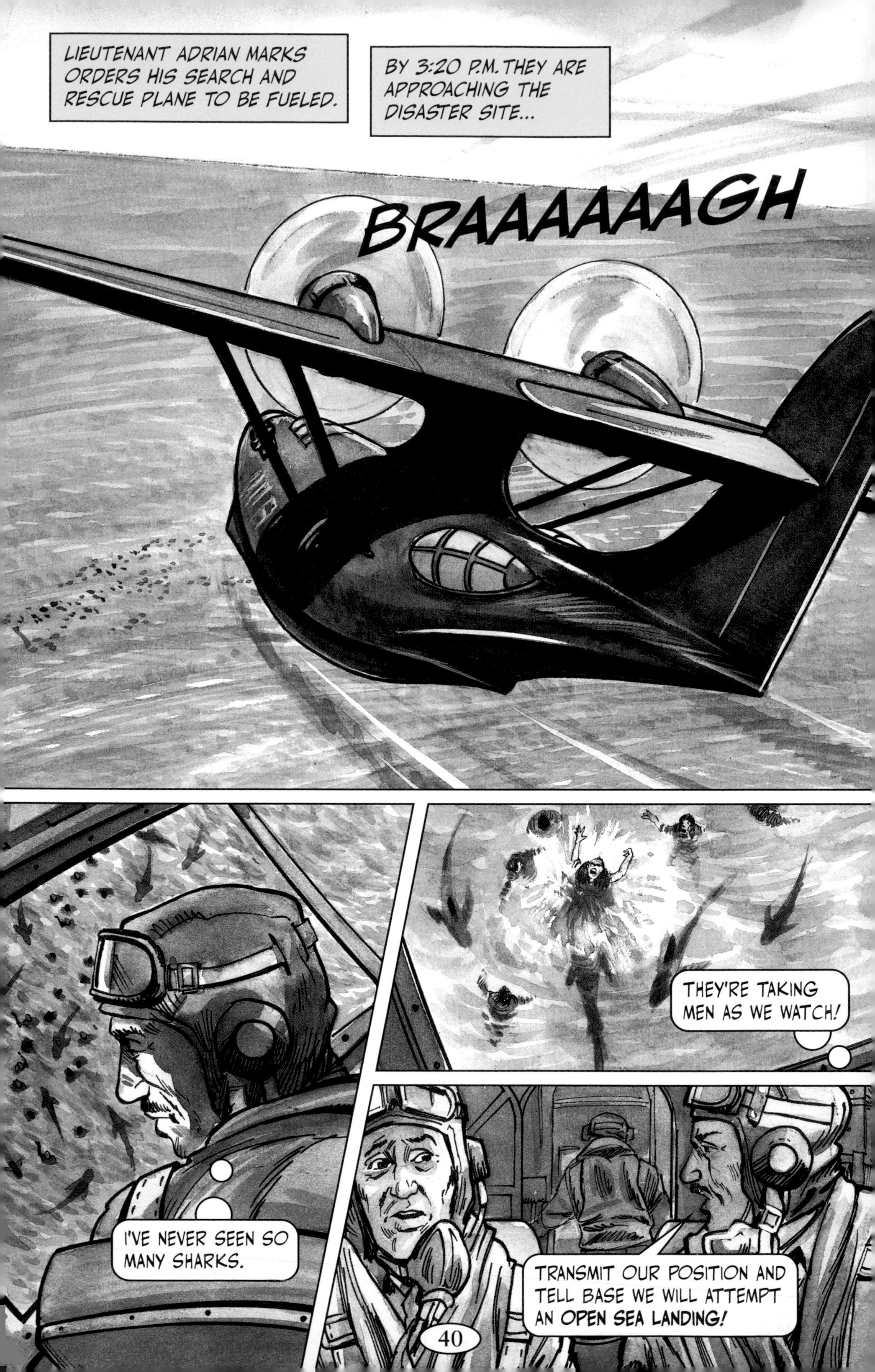
LIEUTENANT ADRIAN MARKS ORDERS HIS SEARCH AND RESCUE PLANE TO BE FUELED.
BY 3:20 P.M. THEY ARE APPROACHING THE DISASTER SITE...
BRAAAAAAGH
I'VE NEVER SEEN SO MANY SHARKS.
THEY'RE TAKING MEN AS WE WATCH!
TRANSMIT OUR POSITION AND TELL BASE WE WILL ATTEMPT AN **OPEN SEA LANDING!**

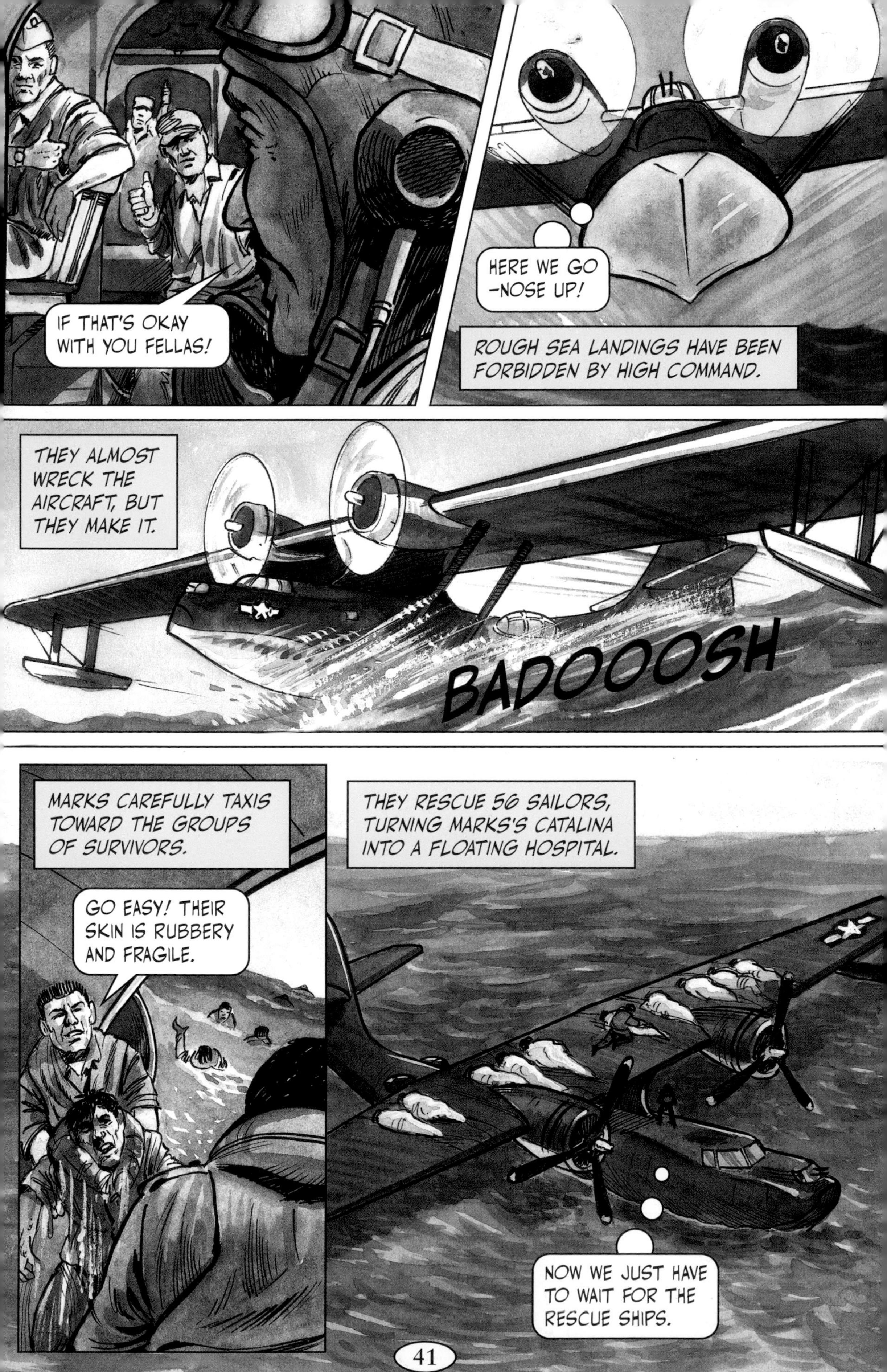
IF THAT'S OKAY WITH YOU FELLAS!
HERE WE GO —NOSE UP!
ROUGH SEA LANDINGS HAVE BEEN FORBIDDEN BY HIGH COMMAND.
THEY ALMOST WRECK THE AIRCRAFT, BUT THEY MAKE IT.
BADOOOSH
MARKS CAREFULLY TAXIS TOWARD THE GROUPS OF SURVIVORS.
GO EASY! THEIR SKIN IS RUBBERY AND FRAGILE.
THEY RESCUE 56 SAILORS, TURNING MARKS'S CATALINA INTO A FLOATING HOSPITAL.
NOW WE JUST HAVE TO WAIT FOR THE RESCUE SHIPS.

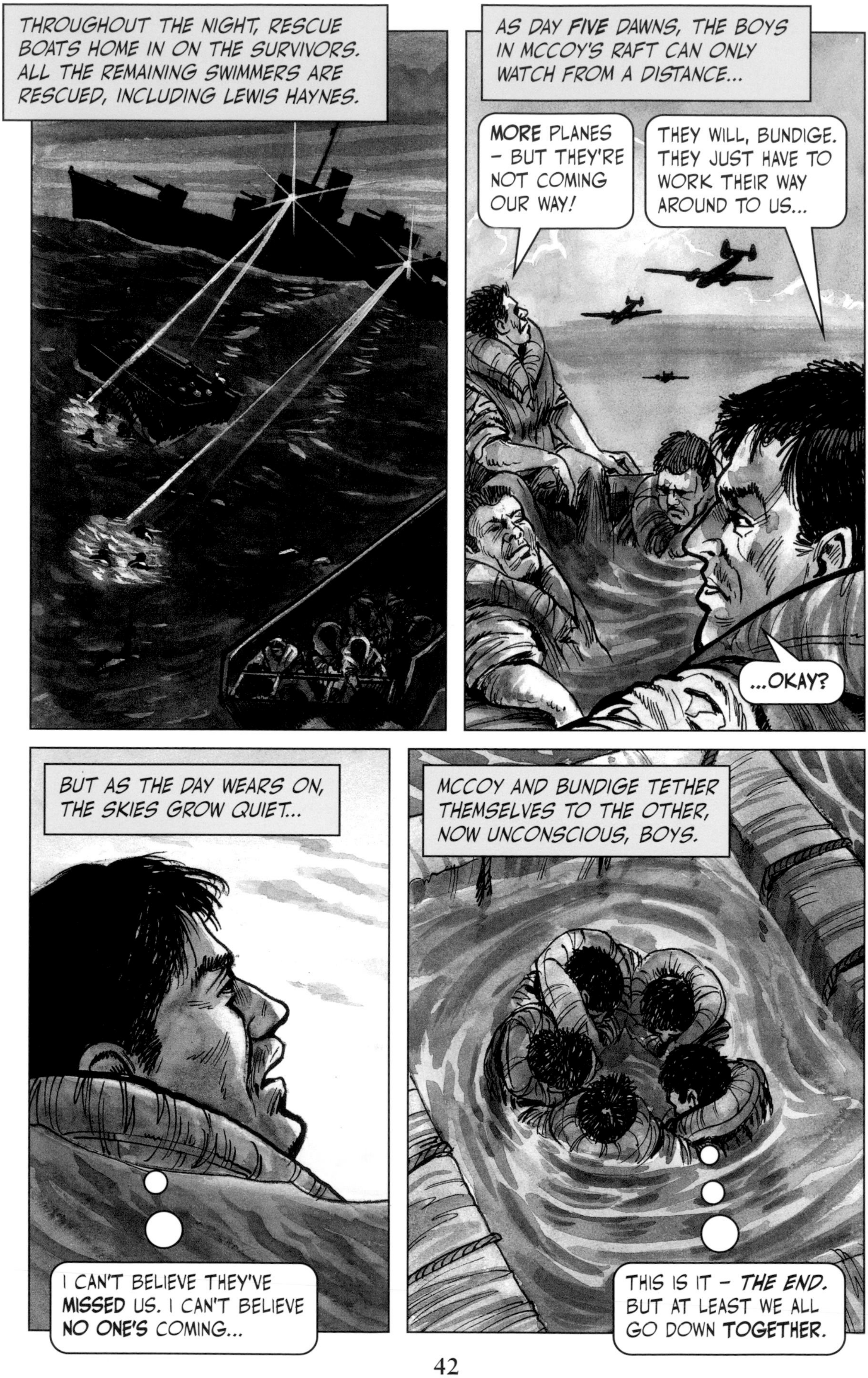
THROUGHOUT THE NIGHT, RESCUE BOATS HOME IN ON THE SURVIVORS. ALL THE REMAINING SWIMMERS ARE RESCUED, INCLUDING LEWIS HAYNES.
AS DAY FIVE DAWNS, THE BOYS IN MCCOY'S RAFT CAN ONLY WATCH FROM A DISTANCE...
MORE PLANES – BUT THEY'RE NOT COMING OUR WAY!
THEY WILL, BUNDIGE. THEY JUST HAVE TO WORK THEIR WAY AROUND TO US...
...OKAY?
BUT AS THE DAY WEARS ON, THE SKIES GROW QUIET...
I CAN'T BELIEVE THEY'VE MISSED US. I CAN'T BELIEVE NO ONE'S COMING...
MCCOY AND BUNDIGE TETHER THEMSELVES TO THE OTHER, NOW UNCONSCIOUS, BOYS.
THIS IS IT – THE END. BUT AT LEAST WE ALL GO DOWN TOGETHER.

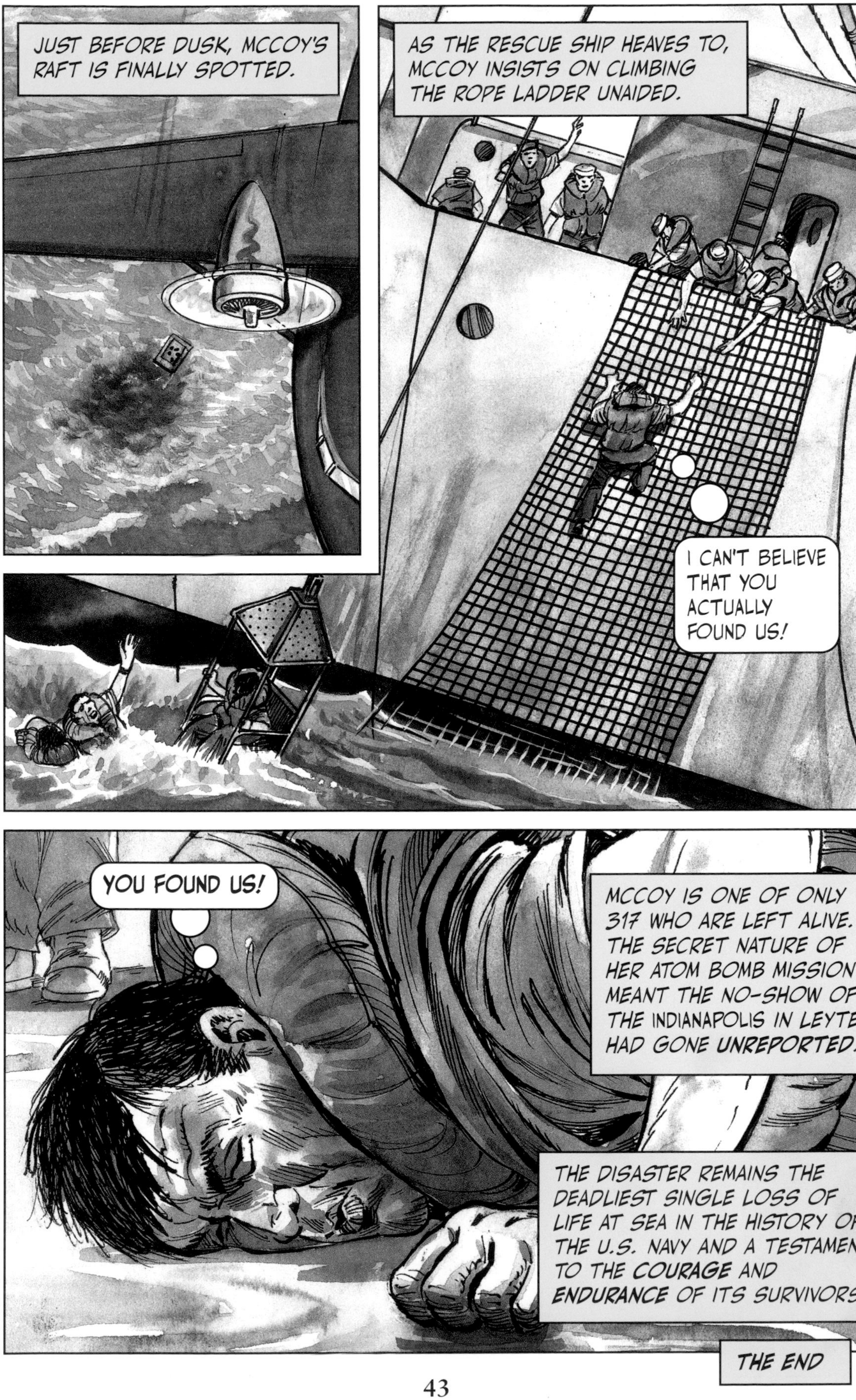
JUST BEFORE DUSK, MCCOY'S RAFT IS FINALLY SPOTTED.
AS THE RESCUE SHIP HEAVES TO, MCCOY INSISTS ON CLIMBING THE ROPE LADDER UNAIDED.
I CAN'T BELIEVE THAT YOU ACTUALLY FOUND US!
YOU FOUND US!
MCCOY IS ONE OF ONLY 317 WHO ARE LEFT ALIVE. THE SECRET NATURE OF HER ATOM BOMB MISSION MEANT THE NO-SHOW OF THE INDIANAPOLIS IN LEYTE HAD GONE UNREPORTED.
THE DISASTER REMAINS THE DEADLIEST SINGLE LOSS OF LIFE AT SEA IN THE HISTORY OF THE U.S. NAVY AND A TESTAMENT TO THE COURAGE AND ENDURANCE OF ITS SURVIVORS.
THE END

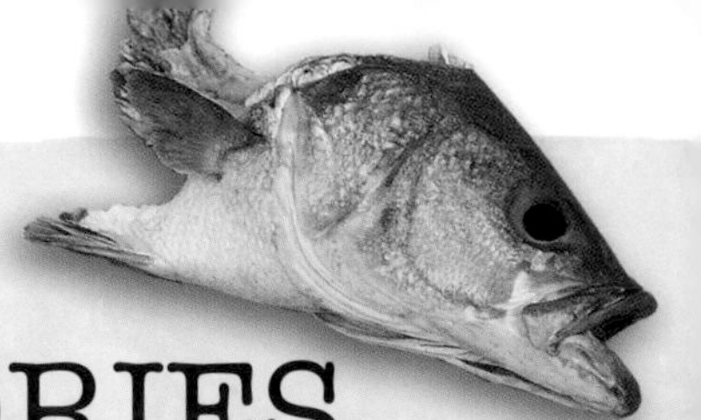

MORE OCEAN SURVIVAL STORIES

The ocean is to be feared and respected. Sea conditions can change suddenly and without warning. Encounters with ocean creatures, human error, or simple mechanical failure can leave people unexpectedly stranded in its vastness...

THE TRAGEDY OF THE *ESSEX*, SOUTH PACIFIC, NOVEMBER 1820

Captained by 29-year-old George Pollard, the Nantucket whaling ship *Essex* had spent the past nine months successfully, and uneventfully, hunting for sperm whales in the South Pacific.

On November 20, a school of whales was sighted. First Mate Owen Chase's boat was damaged in the pursuit, and he brought it back to the ship for repairs. While hammering on the deck, he noticed a huge dark shape, some 85 ft (26 m) long, swimming near the ship. As the crew looked on, the shape charged.

The sperm whale struck the ship twice, holing the bow below the waterline. The deck began to drop. Grabbing everything they could, Chase and his crewmen quickly launched their repaired whaler. Minutes later the *Essex* keeled over. The others returned. The survival of all 20 men now depended on making a journey to the coast of South America, 2,300 miles (3,700 km) to the east, in three small whaleboats, without adequate provisions.

At first things went well. The rations seemed to be lasting, and they even found a small island on which three men elected to stay behind. By the turn of the new year they had done a quarter of the trip and were living on half rations. The 17 formerly tired and hungry men became exhausted, starving, and desperate...

On January 10 the first man died and was buried at sea. The next day a sudden rainstorm separated Chase's boat from the other two. Two more men died in Chase's boat. Rather than succumb to starvation, they decided to eat the second man. In the other boats, Pollard and his men made the same grisly decision, even drawing lots to see who would be sacrificed. In all, only five survived to be rescued from the boats. The story of the *Essex* became a cause célèbre and inspired the novel *Moby Dick*.

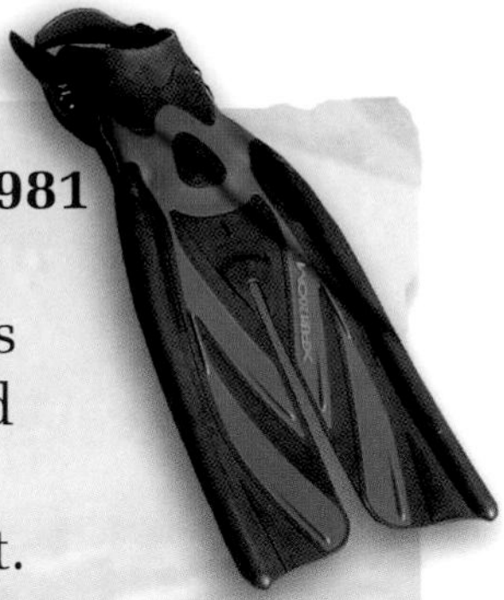

Swimming for Life off North Carolina, November 1981

How long could you survive in 59°F (15°C) water without survival clothing? The U.S. Coast Guard says less than two hours. As her light aircraft sank around her, pilot Kathy Maready knew she had less than 30 seconds before she was going to have to face that test.

It had all seemed so routine, a short flight home from scuba training on Lady Island, N.C. Then the Cessna's engine had unexpectedly cut out over the coast, five minutes from landing. Maready had guided the little aircraft to a textbook landing on the ocean. As she swam free and watched the blinking taillight spiral down into the depths below, her fight for survival began.

As she swam toward the distant shore, her body began to seize up. Thoughts of death welled up in Maready's mind. She focused on the people she loved. The emotion helped warm her. Through a superhuman effort, Maready swam for seven and a half hours until she reached the shore. After being rescued she was hospitalized for three days with acute hypothermia, but recovered—a testament to her personal fitness and will to live.

Adrift on the North Atlantic, February 1982

American naval architect and sailor Steven Callahan was in despair. Six days out of the Canary Islands his self-designed sloop *Napoleon Solo* had sunk after collision with a whale. Having crossed two sea lanes and the paths of seven ships that refused to stop, he concluded that he was going to have to rescue himself.

His only comfort, other than the tiny inflatable raft he was in, was a school of fish that had been following him for days. They were tasty dorado, and occasionally one of the rainbow-hued fish would come near enough for Callahan to spear it for food. He had solar stills to purify water and a survival manual, but was frustrated that he couldn't sail his raft.

He followed a daily routine of exercise, getting water, and fishing. He also mused on his "home" and how it might be improved. Eventually he was seen by fishermen near the island of Guadeloupe, after 76 days at sea. Callahan went on to design a new type of sailable survival raft.

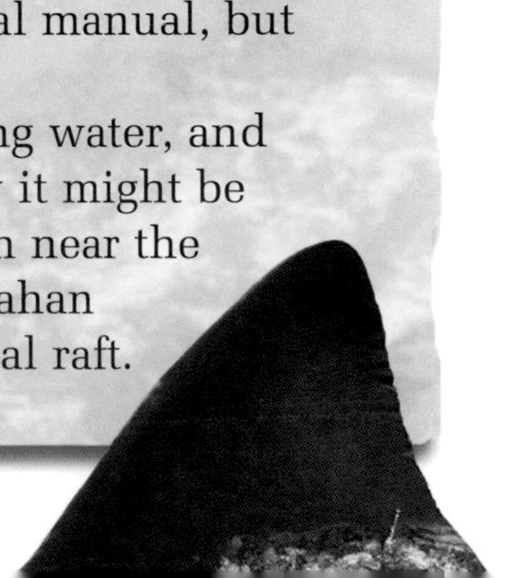

GLOSSARY

bailing Scooping water out of a boat to stop it sinking.

barnacle Marine crustacean with an external shell, which attaches itself to the undersides of boats.

bow The front part of the hull of a ship or boat.

breadfruit The large, round, starchy fruit of a tropical tree.

buoy A device designed to float on the water.

caustic A substance that can burn or destroy living tissue.

cephalopods A class of active predatory sea creatures comprising octopuses, squids, and cuttlefish.

crustaceans A large group of mainly aquatic invertebrates that includes crabs, lobsters, shrimps, and barnacles.

debris The remains of something that has been destroyed.

dehydration The loss of a large amount of water from the body.

ecosystem A biological community of interacting organisms and their physical environment.

equator An imaginary line drawn around the Earth, equally distant from both poles, which divides the Earth into northern and southern halves.

gorges To eat until one feels sick.

heave to To stop moving.

hypothermia Condition of having an abnormally low body temperature, typically one that is life-threateningly low.

keel A long, thin piece of wood or metal along the bottom of a boat, that helps it to balance in the water.

metabolism The chemical processes that occur within a living organism in order to maintain life.

mutiny A refusal by a group of sailors or soldiers to accept someone's authority or command.

paramount Of overriding importance.

quarterdeck The back part of a ship's upper deck, where the officers often live.

scavengers A creature that eats anything it can find.

sextant A piece of equipment that sailors use for looking at the stars so that they can calculate the position of their ship.

singe To burn something slightly so that only the edge or surface is affected.

sodium A chemical element, the main constituent of salt. It is toxic to humans in large doses.

spoils The benefit that someone gets when they win something.

stern The back part of a ship.

wake The track left by a vessel in the water.

FOR MORE INFORMATION

ORGANIZATIONS

Association for Rescue at Sea (AFRAS), Inc
PO Box 565
Fish Creek
WI 4212-0565
920 743 5434
Web site: http://www.afras.org

United States Coast Guard
Coast Guard Headquarters
2100 Second Street, SW
Washington, DC 20593
Web site: http://www.uscg.mil

FOR FURTHER READING

Gaines, Ann. *The Coast Guard in Action* (US Military Branches and Careers). Berkeley Heights, NJ: Enslow, 2001.

Gonzalez, Lissette. *Search and Rescue Specialists* (Dangerous Jobs). New York, NY: Rosen Publishing, 2007.

Lewis, Simon. *Survival at Sea* (Difficult and Dangerous). London, England: Franklin Watts, 2008.

Nelson, Peter. *Left for Dead: A Young Man's Search for Justice for the USS Indianapolis.* New York, NY: Delacorte Books, 2002.

Philbrick, Nathaniel. *Revenge of the Whale: The True Story of the Whaleship Essex.* Kirkwood, NY: Putnam Publishing Group, 2002.

INDEX

Web Sites

Due to the changing nature of Internet links, Rosen Publishing has developed an online list of Web sites related to the subject of this book. This site is updated regularly. Please use this link to access the list:

http://www.rosenlinks.com/ddss/ocea